Painting and Culture of the Mongols

M. S. IPSIROGLU

Painting and Culture of the Mongols

TRANSLATED FROM THE GERMAN WITH AN

INTRODUCTION BY E. D. PHILLIPS

THAMES AND HUDSON · LONDON

Photographs by A. Albeck, H. Krimer and V. Yazan

© HIRMER VERLAG MUNICH 1965

THIS EDITION © THAMES AND HUDSON LONDON 1967

PRINTED IN HOLLAND BY MEIJER WORMERVEER

PLATES PRINTED IN GERMANY BY HIRMER VERLAG MUNICH

TRANSLATOR'S PREFACE

I am delighted to have the opportunity to introduce to a wider, English-speaking readership this intriguing collection of paintings, which has for too long been known only to orientalists. Their remarkably high quality will, I imagine, come as a surprise to all who encounter them for the first time in Professor Ipsiroglu's fascinating book. In this Preface I have thought it desirable to say a little more of the general history of the Saray albums as a collection, so far as this is known or can be conjectured. The subject can be pursued in the references given by the author himself, but it is not treated in detail here. Again, many to whom the book will give pleasure may not know the elaborate backgrounds to the subjects of some illustrations, which come from works of literature still celebrated in countries of Moslem or more particularly of Persian culture. These make up the second part of this Preface. Of other pictures that have caused argument among orientalists themselves, I naturally say much less. In any case they do not illustrate known literature.

Professor Ipsiroglu has done a valuable service by publishing in book form, and often in colour, so distinctive a selection from the miniatures collected in four albums of the Topkapu Saray Library at Istanbul, together with a few of the same kinds from the University Libraries of Istanbul and Tübingen. These unusual pictures, some of them belonging to illuminated manuscripts and others separate and of unknown context, are distinguished from the accompanying hundreds of Persian illustrations, or Turkish imitations of such, by their obviously foreign inspiration. But they have to be judged against the background of Persian art.

Any reader who is acquainted with the major forms of oriental art will see much Chinese influence in some of the pictures; in others he will be reminded of the frescoes of Turfan and generally of the art of Chinese Turkestan, itself a combination of Chinese, Sassanian and Indian traditions on a native foundation; in others again he will see that a fundamentally Persian style has been modified by such details as Mongol faces and Mongol dress in the human figures. The pictures of hitherto unknown demons are much harder to place. The earthy representations of nomads and their beasts seem to show life among the Turks of Iran or more probably of Transoxania or Turkestan; such scenes must have been familiar to anyone who knew these regions, but for us they reveal a world which lies very much in the background of history with a realism that might never have been suspected. The term 'Mongol art' when it is applied to such a variety of styles needs some explanation.

The difference between the various types of art here illustrated and typically Persian or Near Eastern art of the same period is sometimes so great as to suggest that the pictures come from countries northeast of Persia, but there is always the possibility that some were painted in Persia from foreign models. It is known that Chinese art was admired and copied in Persia at least from the Ilkhan period onward.

Those pictures which have a basically Persian character, in spite of their foreign features, are regarded as simply Persian work done under new masters, the Mongols, with special touches to suit their taste. But the scenes of demons seem entirely foreign and are considered akin to Chinese pictures of demons of Taoist origin. Yet they have also an element of caricature, which suggests to some scholars that they are not themselves Central Asian or Far Eastern work, but work done in Persia by artists who had seen these exotic styles from the outside and showed their reaction in this way. This is a different view from Professor Ipsiroglu's. It is not for a translator, however interested, to judge between the experts, but if he writes a Preface he should indicate something of their diverse opinions.

The stretch of Iranian history within which pictures in the albums can be dated is a long one. It begins just before the Mongol conquests early in the thirteenth century, and extends through the rule of the Ilkhans (1258–1336) and of their local successors in various parts of Iran such as the Jala'irs in the west (1336–1411), of Timur and his successors in Iran and Central Asia (1369–1500), and of the later rivals of the Timurids, the Turkman dynasties of the Black Sheep (1378–1469) and the White Sheep (1378–1502), into the first few reigns of the nationalist Safavid Dynasty of Iran, which ruled from 1500 onward and was during the sixteenth century a powerful enemy of the Ottoman Turks. During the whole of that period, Iran was open to various influences from Central and Eastern Asia, but it was the Mongols who created the conditions in which this obtained. It is thus convenient to use their name to cover the diverse types of art which resulted, sooner or later, from their conquests. The effect of their invasion was not merely military and political but cultural. It appears even in such Persian art as does not show the direct influence of the Far East in its style, as these pictures do, because new types of subject were treated, including landscape, and the figure of Mohammed. But the exact nature of the change is made more difficult to define by the destruction resulting from the Mongol invasions, in which Moslem art of the preceding centuries was so extensively destroyed.

During their first invasion under Chingis Khan, which began in 1219, and their occupation of Northern and Eastern Iran from the departure of Chingis, and again during the invasion of Hulagu in 1254 and the reigns of Hulagu and his successors who lived as nomads until the accession in 1281 of Ahmed, the first Ilkhan to embrace Islam, there is little reason to think that Mongol rulers took an interest in Persian art or in altering it to suit themselves. Ahmed's successor Argun (1284–91) was a Buddhist, and during his reign influences of a civilized kind from Central Asia and China should have been particularly strong. But Gazan (1295–1304), who restored Islam as the religion of the state, had a great interest in culture and even in scholarship. Under him the Mongols settled permanently in the cities, and in Tabriz his court attracted foreign scholars from many countries. These scholars, notably the learned Mongol Bolod, the Ching-Hsiang, or political resident sent by Kubilai Khan from Peking, supplied the vizier and universal historian Rashid-ed-Din with much of the information that he used in his *Compendium of World History (Jami-at-Tawarikh)*. Tabriz was the official capital of the Ilkhans, even while they personally lived as nomads, from the accession of Abaka in 1265 until the reign of Oljaitu, who succeeded Gazan. It always remained an important centre of culture and a place where works of art would be collected, even after the library founded by Rashid was destroyed at the time of his execution in 1336. It kept this importance under the Jala'irs, the Timurids, the Turkmans and the Safavids, and is thus likely to be the place where the pictures in the Saray albums were finally collected and where the albums were made up.

6

The four albums catalogued in the Saray Museum as Nos. 2153, 2152, 2154 and 2160 contain pictures of various dates within the period mentioned, but three of them are connected with the names of particular rulers. No. 2153 contains two pictures of the Ottoman Sultan Mehmed the Conqueror (1451–81) and pictures of his date and earlier, so that it could have been made up during the fifteenth century. No. 2152 contains specimens of the handwriting of Ibrahim, governor of Shiraz from 1414 to 1434 and of Baysungur, governor of Tabriz who died in 1433, both sons of Shah Rukh and grandsons of Timur, so that it too could be dated to the fifteenth century. No. 2154, which is particularly Persian in character, contains a statement that its contents were collected in 1544 for Bahram Mirza, brother of the Safavid Shah Tahmasp, who died in 1549. There are no such indications for No. 2160. It was for a time believed in Turkey that all of the albums were made for Mehmed the Conqueror and show the width of his interests as a collector or purchaser, and of his patronage. But at least No. 2154 is too late to be explained in this way. It is just possible that the contents of the three apparently earlier albums were carried off from Tabriz to Istanbul by Sultan Selim I (1512–20) in his war against the Safavids, when he held Tabriz for a short time in 1514. For Selim, like Mehmed, was not only a ruthless fighter but a man of wide culture. If this is so, No. 2154 or its contents must have reached Istanbul in different circumstances. But little can be said to be proved about the history of the albums.

If the Ilkhan period is thought too early for all but a few of the pictures to have been painted in it and is certainly too early for the collections to have been formed in it, the Timurid period on the other hand seems particularly suited for both activities. Timur's empire, ruled from Samarkand, included most of the territory from which the pictures are likely to have come, and his much weaker descendants still ruled kingdoms in Turkestan and in Iran, where they had capitals at such places as Herat and Tabriz. It may be guessed that most of the painting and of the collecting was done during this period when Central Asia and Iran were still ruled by princes of Mongol descent, though now of Turkish speech. If Tabriz was the final place of collection in Iran, it may be remarked that it is near Ottoman territory and was and is inhabited by many Turks, even though these are not Ottoman Turks.

I now pass on to the promised explanations of the subjects of some of the pictures.

The story of Warqa and Gulshah, shown in illustrations 1 and 2, is a complicated tale of frustrated love set in Arabia in the age of Mohammed. A Persian poem on this subject was composed in the eleventh century by a certain 'Ayuqqi' for Mahmud of Ghaznah, the Central Asian Turkish conqueror of Eastern Iran, who was a great patron of Persian literature. The manuscript (Hazine 841) of the Saray Library, to which the pictures belong, is a copy from the thirteenth or fourteenth century. Two tribes of Bedouin, the Banu Shaybah and the Banu Dabyah, were encamped near Mecca. The chiefs of the Banu Shaybah were two brothers, Hilal and Humam. Hilal had a daughter named Gulshah and Humam a son named Warqa. They were educated together until Warqa became an accomplished warrior and Gulshah a beautiful and highly cultured girl. They fell in love, and when they were sixteen years old their parents prepared to marry them.

But before the contract was completed, Rabi b'Adnan of the Banu Dabyah, who had already asked without success for Gulshah's hand, carried her off in a raid. He fell more in love with her than ever, and she did not refuse him outright, but asked for a delay of a week before marriage. The Banu Shaybah next attacked the Banu Dabyah in a bloody battle. Rabi killed Warqa's father and was then furiously attacked by Warqa himself. Gulshah escaped from Rabi's tent and hastened, armed and mounted, to the battlefield with her face covered. Warqa's horse slipped, so that he was at the mercy of Rabi, who did not kill him but took him prisoner. Gulshah then uncovered her face, Rabi was delighted, thinking that she had come to admire him. But she killed him with a lance thrust and delivered Warqa. This is the moment depicted in illustration 2. After this, to cut a long story short, the lovers were separated again by many misfortunes in the Yemen and in Damascus, and never reunited for more than a moment, until both died of grief.

The scenes from Firdausi's *Shahname* are of incidents from the remotest mythical or legendary past mentioned in Iranian tradition, belonging, in so far as they are history, to eastern Iran of the time before Cyrus the Great founded the Persian Empire. Firdausi himself lived under Mahmud of Ghaznah, and used this ancient material.

Illustration 3 shows the hero Isfandiyar, son of King Gushtasp, in battle with a dragon which has swallowed one of his chariot horses and seems likely to swallow him. It was during Gushtasp's reign that Zoroaster appeared, and he was the first king to embrace the Zoroastrian faith. Isfandiyar, commanding his father's army against the kings of Turan, traversed all countries, spreading the Zoroastrian faith, and after many adventures died fighting Rustam, a still greater hero. Among his adventures were battles against monsters such as this dragon. He attacked it in a chariot fitted with projecting sword-blades and with a strong protective chamber of wood carried on top, in which he sat as driver. The dragon swallowed the horses, but the chariot with its blades stuck in its throat and drew blood. Isfandiyar climbed out of his chamber and split the dragon's skull with a blow of his sword, but then he fainted with the poison that the dragon exhaled.

Illustration 4 shows another of his adventures, a battle with the Simurgh, a giant bird (the original of the roc of the *Arabian Nights*) which could carry an elephant in its claws. Isfandiyar sallied forth against this creature too with the same equipment. The Simurgh was pierced with the sword blades and lost strength until Isfandiyar climbed out and cut it to pieces.

Illustration 5, portraying the four loyal companions of Kai Khusrau, takes a dramatic moment following the king's disappearance. Kai Khusrau, the greatest king of the legendary Kayanid dynasty, declared at the end of his reign that he would go into the mountains never to be seen again, and would leave the throne to his son Luhrasp. He went with eight heroes, of whom four left him, as they were ordered, but four would not, namely Tus, Giv, Feriburz and Bijen. After they had stopped by a spring for the night, he bade them farewell for ever, saying that when the sun rose he would be gone. He told them not to stay in the mountains, for a great storm would come with heavy snow and would hinder them from finding their way back to Iran. They fell asleep sadly and found next morning that he had disappeared. They stayed to look for him and did not find him, but returned to the spring and lay down again to sleep. The storm swept down on them as they slept and covered them with snow, so that they died. They were found dead by Rustam and the army.

Concerning illustration 6, showing the birth of Rustam, one or two details may be added. The Simurgh appears here in a benevolent role. The bird came to the help of Zal when he burned one of its feathers which it had given him to summon it at need. For the operation it advised that Rustam's mother should be made drunk with wine and spells. The operation was done with a sword and the wound immediately sewn up. A herb crushed in milk and musk was put on the wound and healed it at once.

Prince Siyawush, who is seen in illustration 7 undergoing ordeal by fire, was the son of King Kai Kaus. He was charged with attempting the virtue of the Queen, his stepmother, who was enamoured of his supernatural beauty and tempted him without success. He had to pass through a great flame, riding his black horse and wearing a golden helmet. He was unharmed, and thus proved innocent. Later he fought, like other princes, against Afrasiab, King of Turan, but eventually he made peace, married Afrasiabs' daughter and built the fabulous ring-walled city of Kangdiz. But he was calumniated again, and murdered by Afrasiab. He was avenged by his son Kai Khusrau, who conquered Turan.

Gayumart, who appears in illustration 12 as the first king, is said in the *Shahname* to have ruled for thirty years in this capacity and as ruler of the world, establishing his dwelling in the mountains and dressing himself and his people in tiger-skins. He invented civilization and all its arts, including clothing. He shone like the sun. All the wild animals in the world ran to him and bowed before his throne to receive his laws. In Zoroastrian belief he had also been the first man, and his name meant 'dying life'. He was created by the good god Ormuzd and killed by the evil god Ahriman. He seems to be derived ultimately from another mythological figure, Yima, a being who was in Zoroastrian belief first man and first king, and in fact a god who took on mortality. Yima made a paradise on earth for a thousand years with unfailing food and drink, in which men animals and plants never grew old. He then disappeared under the earth, but is destined to reappear. Something of the original god still clings to Gayumart in this illustration, for he has the aureole of a supernatural being and the air of ruling creation, like Adam before the Fall.

Also from the *Shahname* is the subject of illustration 50, the fight between Iskandar and the tusked wolves. Alexander the Great became the subject of the widespread *Alexander Romance*, which originated soon after his death in a Graeco-Egyptian milieu at Alexandria and spread in various versions throughout Asia and Europe during later antiquity and the Middle Ages. Alexander became an admired figure in Jewish, Christian and Moslem tradition, being credited with exploits and wanderings far beyond his historical achievements. Many tales which had been told of older heroes became attached to him. Through the popularity of the *Romance*, which was even translated into Pahlavi in Iran, Alexander or Iskandar was received as a hero into the tradition eventually used by Firdausi, though the Zoroastrian tradition of older Iran had dismissed him in a few allusions as an impious destroyer. In the *Shahname* he is adopted into the royal line, which historically he overthrew in the person of Darius III, by the invention of his birth by a daughter of King Failakus, who represents his father Philip of Macedon, to Dara, King of Persia. Dara repudiated her and married another wife, by whom he had Darab or Darius III. In this version Iskandar in conquering Persia merely overthrows his half-brother and continues the same line. Iskandar even revives the glories of the legendary past after a period less interesting, though historical, reigns. For his career, as described in the *Romance* and taken over in summary for the *Shahname*, is much like those of the legendary Kayanids. Like Isfandiyar, he is made to explore unknown regions and fight personally against such monsters as the tusked wolves.

The battle of the crows and the owls shown in illustration 17 is a well-known episode from *Kalila and Dimna*, an Indian book of animal fables intended for the instruction of rulers. It was compiled about AD 300 but presented as tales told by the Brahmin Bidpai to Dabshelim, an Indian king of the generation following Alexander's Indian campaign. The book is named after the story of the jackals Kalila and Dimna who were in the service of the lion, the king of beasts, but this episode is not really connected with them. On a great mountain there lived two rival hosts of birds: a thousand crows nesting in a many-branched tree and a thousand owls living in holes in the rock. Each host had its king, and they were enemies. The owls made a treacherous attack by night on the sleeping crows and killed many of them. After some time, during which they debated and sent their vizier as a spy, the crows in their turn attacked by day while the owls were asleep. They gathered dry sticks, placed them by the owls' burrows, lit them and fanned the fire with their wings, as in the picture. The owls were either suffocated by the smoke or, if they came out, perished in the flames. The moral is that rulers should be well informed of the circumstances and designs of their enemies. *Kalila and Dimna* is said to have been translated into Pahlavi before the Moslem conquest of Iran, and was certainly translated later into Arabic and thence into medieval Persian.

It is unnecessary to lengthen this Preface by remarks on the illustrations of subjects from the *Koran*, which are fully explained by Professor Ipsiroglu. In any case, translations of the *Koran* are many and easily found.

For further reading on the background of this book the following historical sources or treatments of sources are suggested: Sir Henry Yule and H. Cordier, *Cathay and the Way Thither*, being a collection of medieval notices of China, London (Hakluyt Society), 1915 (2nd ed.), 4 vols. *The Travels of Ibn Battuta*, transl. H. A. R. Gibb, London (Hakluyt Society), 1958–62, 2 vols. E. Bretschneider, *Medieval Researches from East Asiatic Sources*, London, 1887, 2 vols. L. Olschki, *Marco Polo's Asia*, Los Angeles, 1960, M. Bussagli, *Painting of Central Asia*, London, 1963. (This is on the Uighur and other non-Chinese painting which may be among the sources for Mongol painting.)

For Firdausi's *Shahname* see the translation of Jules Mohl in seven volumes: *Le Livre des Rois*, Paris. Imprimerie Nationale 1876–78; and for *Kalila and Dimna*, *Anvari-Suhaili* (the Persian version of the *Fables of Pilpay* (Bidpai) by Husain Va'iz U'l Kashiji) translated into prose and verse by Edward B. Eastwick, Hertford, Stephen Austen, 1854. All other material used is already mentioned in Professor Ipsiroglu's notes.

E. D. PHILLIPS

10

INTRODUCTION

Only two of the pictures reproduced in this book belong to the pre-Mongol Seljuk period; the rest come from the Mongol era of the 14th century, which lasted longer than the Mongol dominion and *1, 2* extended as far as the Timurid period, that is, to the beginning of the 15th century. The Mongol world-empire was divided into separate realms of great size: the territories of the Golden Horde, that is to say Kipchak Russia, also Iran and Persia, Chagatai Turkestan, and finally the eastern empire of Yuan China.

One group of pictures in this book, which, following the traditional terminology, we call Persian-Mongol, shows the marks of a western origin in Persia and neighbouring lands. In this group we are dealing with works which arise from the interaction of eastern and western currents of culture and therefore show in a great or less degree a unique mixture of influences. In their style these pictures are *3–7, 11–26, 50* unmistakably dependent on the great Far Eastern and Central Asian traditions of painting which the Mongols carried westward. The western share is rather confined to the iconography of the figures. The Near East at this time had a highly developed literature in Arabic and Persian, and the painting of the Mongol period drew its favourite themes from works belonging to this literature. In this way the foundation was laid for Islamic illustration of books. The illustration of the Persian national epic *Shah-name (The Book of Kings)* by Firdausi, done about 1300, marked a decisive turning point in the development which was to lead away from pre-Mongol Mesopotamian art to the new Mongol style. *3–7*

In the second quarter of the 14th century appeared the earliest illustrations of the ascension *(Mi'raj)* of Mohammed. Until this time religious themes in Islamic lands were subject to the unwritten ban on illustration. The portrayals of the prophet's ascension to Heaven are evidence that under the Mongols figural representation enjoyed unlimited freedom, which was bound to encourage the development of the illustrated book in the Islamic East. *19–24*

The remaining material in our book can be fitted without difficulty into the so-called Chinese-Mongol *8–10, 27–49, 51–54* group of styles. Western iconography plays a very small part in this group, so that themes of East Asian origin, above all in the illustration of fairy tales and in representations taken from Buddhist belief, are all the more prominent. But this should not mislead us into moving the original home of these pictures to China. No effect worth mentioning in the artistic life of the eastern empire can be assigned to the Mongol conquerors: in contrast, the countries of the Near East, Persia above all, were in the Mongol period the scene of cultural events of some importance. The illustrations to Rashid-ed-Din's *World Chronicle* were produced in Tabriz. Other cultural centres to be considered for the origin of Mongol painting in the Near East were Shiraz, Herat and Baghdad.

A large number of pictures, whose themes come from a background entirely strange to townsmen, deserve special mention within this group. They represent scenes from the life of the nomads, their tools, *29–47* weapons and beasts, and terrifying demon figures, rites of conjuration, scenes of worship and sacrifice, which seem to have some connection with shamanism. These representations are the only documents in the form of pictures which give us any information about the world of the nomad peoples of the steppes. The pictures vary in size and in technical accomplishment. It can hardly be assumed that they are book-painting, that is to say, illustrations to a manuscript. It may be conjectured that some of them are based on dramatic performances, that is, on the text recited. In the rest we have more or less the products of a

44-45 naturalistic school of art which may be supposed to have drawn its themes directly from reality.

The style of these pictures, which form a self-contained group, is distinguished by a distinct linearity and a manner of expression strongly influenced by drawing. In most of the pictures we can detect the hand of a master of whose personality we know nothing. Some of his pictures are signed 'Ustad Mehmed Siyah Qalem—Master Mehmed, the Black Pen'. Since the artists of the east keep their personalities anonymous, we seldom find signed work there. Where there is a signature, the names are not so prominently and awkwardly written as they are in our pictures. Further, it often happens in the east that an artist calls himself in his signature 'the lowest of slaves', but never that he calls himself 'master'. So we have here certainly not a real name but an ascription dating from a later period. The compound 'Siyah Qalem—Black Pen' stands for a technique of drawing in the execution of the pictures and is added to the name Mehmed—really a first name—as a nickname. The powerful and expressive manner of drawing in these pictures probably gave rise to this very unusual designation 'Black Pen'. So we find here, apart from a few monochrome drawings, paintings which are dominated by the three colours red, blue and brown. But colour in these pictures is, to a degree otherwise unusual in art of the Chinese-Mongol line of development, subordinated to line and serves only to increase its effect, so that the designation Siyah Qalem is entirely intelligible. The name 'Mehmed Siyah Qalem', then, indicates a definite technique of execution in the works of an unknown master and, it may be guessed, of some minor followers of his. But it must not be forgotten that there are pictures in the Siyah Qalem group which are not signed and that conversely we find pictures elsewhere which bear the name 'Mehmed Siyah Qalem' but do not belong to this group. Thus in identifying a picture by Siyah Qalem we must be guided not by the later ascription but by the style of the artist.

Art-historians of fifty years ago claimed that these pictures, which are so clearly marked off, above all iconographically, from the Islamic west, originated in Kipchak Russia or in the Crimea. Today they are more inclined to trace their origin to Transoxania or Turkestan.[1] Since no work of such a school of painting has yet come to our knowledge from Kipchak, the first suggestion must for the present remain an unproved hypothesis. In favour of an origin from Turkestan are not only the human type shown in these pictures but also the bell-shaped headdresses, which are pointed out likewise in the publications of Aurel Stein and Albert von Le Coq.[2] In Siyah Qalem's pictures and those of his circle we have a movement in art which may be reckoned among the most distinctive productions of Turco-Mongol painting.

Though Mongol painting is strongly influenced from the Far East, the poetry and the impressionistic lyricism of East Asian painting are strange to it. The Mongols love a crystal-clear view and avoid the painter's effects of Chinese art. The refined sense of line, a trait they owe to the Chinese masters, produces in their art a form of modelling which, in the service of a brutal realism, tries to establish well marked plastic and spatial values. This lends to the works of the Mongol painters a sculptural monumentality that

12

suggests closeness to nature and an earth-bound quality. Any feeling for the supra-sensible seems to have been entirely lacking in the Mongols. Thus the wonderful visions of Mohammed on his ascent to Heaven are rendered in Mongol painting as natural events subject to earthly laws. Apart from the wings, nothing *19–24* in the solid build of the Mongol angels in these pictures gives a hint that we are in the presence of heavenly beings, and the demon figures of such a painter as Siyah Qalem are in their nature and gestures so nearly human, that the supernatural in the form of animal or demon attributes rests like a mask on their bodies. It is hard to understand how the art, being so closely linked to this world, could get any foothold in the lands of Islam, which were so deeply permeated by belief in the after-life. Such delight in this world was not normal for Islam. But at first there was no awareness of the danger. The alien character of this art even evoked among the conquered a kind of admiration, and when the victors embraced Islam about 1300, artistic life was frankly overpowered by the Mongol style. This did not change until the fifteenth century, and we see how under the Timurids Mongol realism begins to be dissolved by the decorative tastes of Islamic miniature painting. The Mongol style begins to provoke in Islamic lands a violent reaction, due to a difference in fundamental feeling for the world, to which many of its works must have fallen victim. From the Mongol period we possess no more than a few illustrated manuscripts. We know of the existence of the rest only from a few illustrated pages which have been preserved into our own age in the miscellaneous collection of the Saray albums.[3] We do not know what perished. The work of destruction was no doubt concentrated on those works which particularly displayed the triumph of the pagan Mongol spirit. In such pictures as those of Siyah Qalem, Islam certainly scented the danger of idolatry. That explains why so little of this kind of painting is preserved. The paintings of Siyah Qalem and some few of the minor figures that succeeded him are the sole remnants that have reached us, as if by a miracle.[4]

Because of the inadequate material now at our disposal, any attempt to reconstruct the history of Mongol painting cannot be more than partially successful. But the picture that we get enables us to speak of an artistic movement of which we are only now beginning to understand the importance. In the Mongol period, as in the time of Alexander the Great, the countries of Western Asia awoke to new life under the influence of an alien culture. Time-honoured moulds of set tradition were shattered in this age and free play was allowed to all the influences of the world, a process which unimaginably enriched the life of art. Thanks to the collections in a few Saray albums which have been opened in recent years to scholarly study we are now very well informed about the vigorous activity in art that belongs to the 14th century.[5] To judge by the various fragments of the *Shahname* preserved in these albums, there must have been more than a dozen styles of painting that originated in this century and show a production that spread to the remotest provinces. A new distillation comes from the work of this period, one of new beginnings, which could not be conceived apart from the late antique tradition of painting in Central Asia, and justifies us in speaking of an end of the Middle Ages and a budding Renaissance in the east as well.

But in the 15th century this most promising development has no continuation. Miniature painting under the Timurids does indeed receive from it a few powerful impulses, but what can be traced back later to Mongol painting is really no more than the pale reflection of a great age already forgotten.

The picture of the Mongols that survives to-day in the mind of a cultured European is derived, odd though it may be, even now from the age when Europe was immediately threatened by the Mongol peril.

To-day still many regard the Mongols as a wild and warlike horde from the steppes, that invaded the lands of ancient culture and destroyed them without being able to replace anything that had been annihilated. The fact that this people created the greatest world-empire in history and were able to maintain it for centuries because of their admirable organization must warn us to be cautious in our judgments. Certainly the Mongols had destroyed states and peoples and devastated seats of civilization. But this frenzy of destruction was equalled by their determination in construction. Towns such as Baghdad, which during the founding of the empire had been nearly levelled to the ground, could be restored in a short time under the rule of Chingis' successors. Karakorum developed during the Mongol period into a flourishing royal capital and the new town of Sultaniye was a creation of Mongol builders in the west. New foundations, still traceable in Peking, appeared above all in China. The Mongols opened up the land routes from the Far East to Europe which had been closed for a thousand years. Postal communications in Gazan's time were so organized that news from the most distant points in the empire could reach its ruler in three days. East and west never came into such close contact as at that time, and on this foundation a structure of civilization was raised which we can call imperial Mongol civilization. All these facts must be taken into consideration, if we are to have the right approach to Mongol painting. So in this book the main portion, on Mongol painting, is preceded by a chapter which attempts a survey of Mongol civilization. In such attempts our only sure protection against prejudices is in closely following the historical sources. But on the early history of the Mongols we lack contemporary Mongol writings. The only Mongol tradition preserved from the age when the empire was founded is the *Secret History of the Mongols*, which was translated some twenty years ago into German.[6] We are better off with the later histories from Buddhist-Chinese and Moslem circles, but these leave much to be desired in authenticity and closeness to origins. Among the European sources, names such as Plano Carpini, William Rubruk, John of Montecorvino and Marco Polo are the best known in western countries. The descriptions of Carpini and Rubruk, on which we shall often depend in our account, are without a doubt among the most trustworthy sources left to us by the Christian Middle Ages. Both men spent time as missionaries in Mongolia, and were moreover charged by Pope Innocent IV and Saint Louis to report accurately on conditions there. Thus their descriptions give the first reports by European eye-witnesses on East Asia and provide important confirmation and supplementation of native accounts.

It is my pleasant duty to express here my gratitude to all who have helped me in preparing this book. My thanks are due in the first place to Mr H. Örs, Director of the Topkapu Saray Museum and to Dr W. Gebhardt, Director of the University Library, Tübingen, who gave me access to the valuable works in their collections and permitted me to reproduce them. Nor have I lacked help from my closest colleagues in these studies. I particularly wish to thank the late Professor E. Kühnel, the Nestor of Oriental art-history, and Dr R. Ettinghausen, whose friendly support and expert assistance I was always able to enjoy during the final years. Mr and Mrs Geerken of the Oriental Seminar at Tübingen have very kindly read through the entire manuscript, for which I warmly thank them. I should also like to thank Professor Max Hirmer, the editor and publisher of the original German edition, *Malerei der Mongolen*, and his son Mr Albert Hirmer, who magnanimously met all my wishes, particularly over the number of coloured reproductions; and now Mr E. D. Phillips, who has rendered my text into English.

AN AUDIENCE WITH THE GREAT KHAN

On the 31st May 1254 the Great Kahn Mungge[7] received the Franciscan William of Rubruk, who was at this time staying in Mongolia at the express wish of Louis IX, Saint Louis, of France. Rubruk tells us the details of this audience very fully in his book *Journey to the Mongols* 1253–55 which undoubtedly provides one of the most trustworthy medieval accounts of the Mongols.[8] Mungge Khan then ruled over the newly created Mongol empire which, while it had not yet assumed the size envisaged by, Chingis Khan[9] none the less reached from the Far East across the entire continent of Asia and on across the Urals into Europe, and was thus the greatest empire in history.

When Rubruk was led into the tent of Mungge Khan, he found him, attired in a magnificent robe of fur, reclining on his bed; before this the friar, in his official habit barefooted and bareheaded, had to bend the knee. A few days earlier Mungge Khan had promoted a religious disputation, in which Rubruk had taken part along with the representatives of different faiths. The Confession of Faith made at the Mass 'Credo in unum Deum—I believe in one God,' was the subject of the discussion. When Mungge saw the Franciscan, he came back to this subject. The words that he uttered were noted by Rubruk in the following account:

> 'We Mongols believe that there is only one God in whom we live, and our hearts are turned toward him.' Therefore I said, 'It must be God who grants that; for without his grace no such thing can happen.' And he asked what I had said. The interpreter told him, and he continued, 'But as God has given different fingers to one hand, so he has given to men different ways of being blessed. God has given you Holy Scripture but you Christians do not follow it. You do not find it said in your Scripture that one shall be permitted to upbraid the other, or do you find it there?' he asked. 'No, my Lord,' I replied, 'but I have explained to you from the first that I desire to quarrel with none.' 'I am not speaking of you,' was his answer, 'in the same way you do not find it in your Scripture that a man may for the sake of money turn away from justice.' 'No, my Lord,' I replied, 'and I certainly did not come to this land to gain money for myself and have often refused it when anyone desired to give it me.' There was a secretary present who testified that I had once refused to accept a *yascot* [or *acsom*, a corruption of *yastuq*, a Turkish word for an ingot of silver], and silken stuffs. 'I am not speaking of that,' he said. 'Thus God gave you Holy Scripture and you do not follow it. He has given us soothsayers and we for our part do what they tell us, and live in peace.'[10]

If we wish to understand what these words of the Great Khan meant for Rubruk and the Christian world, we must look back and remind ourselves of a few important events of this age.

THE LEGEND OF PRESTER JOHN

For a long time in Europe there was no sort of knowledge of the Mongols, who seemed to their contemporaries to have emerged from Tartarus (the underworld) and hence were named Tartars (correct form: Tatars). The reports which came through Mongol embassies and refugees from Mongolia were thoroughly confused, and quite inadequate for communicating any image of this alien people in the east. The Christian world at this time was struggling hard in its Crusades against the Mohammedans and the attention of the west was turned toward the Caliph rather than the Great Khan.

At this time the curious legend arose of a mighty king in the Far East who was called Prester John and sometimes known by the Biblical name David. This Prester John or King David, who was supposed to be a Christian, seemed to many to be divinely appointed to bring about the doom of Islam and to reconquer the east for the religion of the Saviour. In 1219 Chingis Khan had invaded the realm of the Islamic Kharizmshah (Mohammed V) and had destroyed it. The oriental Christians, who had been severely oppressed by the Mohammedans, breathed again, and when they heard that the Mongols were approaching the Holy Land, they saw in them allies against the common enemy, the Mohammedans. The legend of Prester John took on more definite shapes through these events and their interpretation in Europe, and King David, the deliverer of Christendom, who had really but a phantom life in people's heads, suddenly received concrete form in the person of Chingis Khan. Thus we see how the letter from the Bishop of Acre, Jacob of Vitry, dated April 18th 1221, which contains the earliest Christian account of Chingis Khan and the Mongols, speaks almost exclusively of King David and his soldiers.[11] Though there is much that is obscure and mistaken in its presentation of historical events, it can be clearly recognized that King David can only mean Chingis Khan, whom Christian tradition had made into a Christian and had connected with the legend of Prester John.

The west awoke from these illusions only in the course of the next two decades. Chingis Khan's campaign against Russia and the Volga Bulgars in 1222–23 brought the first disappointment, and doubts arose whether the Mongols were really Christians. If they had so far been regarded as allies of the Christians, an attempt was now made to link them with the Jews. It was rumoured that the Mongols were descended from the ten tribes of Israel who were carried off into captivity, and that the Jews of Germany secretly supplied them with weapons and provisions. The Annals of Marbach or the Chronicle of Albertus Argentinensis report in connection with the narratives of the Mongol invasion something of the same kind: 'In the year 1222 a very great and strong army from the land of the Persians burst out of its borders and marched through the neighbouring provinces. Why they have marched forth or what they have done we do not know: in a short time they returned to their homeland. But they said they wished to go to Cologne and fetch home the bodies of the three wise men from the east, who were of their nation. We know only one thing: that the Jews were fervently delighted with this rumour, clapped their hands, and congratulated themselves that through this some unexpected deliverance might be vouchsafed to them. Therefore they called the king of those hordes the son of David.'[12]

THE EASTERN POLICY OF CHRISTENDOM AND THE MENDICANT FRIARS

The danger threatening from the East was not fully understood until the Mongols in 1241 thrust westward to the gates of Central Europe. In a letter dated 3rd July of that year from the Emperor Frederick II to the King of England the Mongols are called bestial and irreligious: 'They have only one master whom they

16

obey and worship. They call him the God of the earth. They have burst forth from their land to destroy the west and to exterminate the Christian religion.'[13] Pope Innocent IV in 1245 summoned a Council of the Church at Lyon, which was to decide on measures to be taken against the peril immediately threatened by the Mongols. A battle in the open field with the invincible army of the Mongols was to be avoided in any circumstances: such a war would at that time have been a hopeless prospect for the west.

So a different plan was envisaged: if it was now definitely established that the Mongols were no sort of Christians, there was still the possibility of winning them for the faith in the Risen Lord. This would remove the Mongol danger and further, because the Mongols after conversion to Christianity would be engaged in the struggle against the Mohammedans, it would serve to realize the ultimate purpose of the Crusades. It was not merely wishful thinking but sober and cunning calculation that led to these decisions.

The newly created Mendicant Orders in the west, which regarded the preaching of the Gospel to all men as their highest task, offered to Pope Innocent IV and Saint Louis outstanding helpers for the execution of their policy; among these was Rubruk himself. We know little indeed of his life. We know only that he was a Franciscan and a friend of Roger Bacon's and, to judge by his description of his travels, he must have been highly educated and have had a sharply observant eye. Before he undertook his journey to Mongolia he was certainly well informed, in so far as that was possible, about conditions there. A few years earlier his fellow Franciscan John de Plano Carpini had been with the Mongols as ambassador of the Pope.

He too had written a report which in the German translation by F. Risch bears the title *Geschichte der Mongolen und Reisebericht 1245–1247 (History of the Mongols and Report of our Journey)*.[14] In Rubruk's time the book was not yet printed, but we know that Carpini was a loquacious and communicative man and very ready to read from his travel-notes to those who came to him. The descriptions in Carpini were thus certainly known to Rubruk. They showed clearly that Guyuk Khan, Mungge's predecessor, though no Christian, was very well disposed towards the Christians. He is said always to have associated with Christians. In fact both his viziers were Christians; he had Christian counsellors and had others trained to be such.

A LETTER FROM THE COMMANDER ELJIGEDEI

In the meantime something happened which certainly did not escape Rubruk's notice. When Saint Louis of France was in Cyprus, Mongol envoys came and brought him a letter from Eljigedei.[15] Eljigedei was no less than the Mongol marshal whom Guyuk had appointed to the supreme command over the troops in Persia and neighbouring countries. In this letter Louis IX is addressed as 'victorious sword of Christianity' and it was expressly declared that the Mongols thought nothing so important as to help the Christians and to strengthen the hands of Christian kings so that God should grant victory to the armies of the kings of Christendom and cause them to triumph over their opponents, 'the despisers of the Cross'. 'We desire,' Eljigedei wrote, 'that all Christians shall be free from bondage, special levies, forced labour, taxes for maintaining the roads and the like, that they shall enjoy honour and esteem, that no one shall lay hands on their possessions and that ruined churches shall be rebuilt and the prayer-boards shall be struck again, and that no one shall presume to hinder them from praying with untroubled and willing hearts for our empire.' The concluding section of the letter bears one more instruction from the 'King of the Earth' which refers to the internal division of Christendom. Apart from the great conflicts between Rome and Byzantium, the Latin and the Greek Church, there were also in the Near East differences of opinion and division between the Armenian

Christians, the Nestorians, and the Jacobites, who no longer formed any kind of credal unity. 'But because they all worship the Cross,' writes Eljigedei, 'they are for us all one. So we request that the illustrious King make no distinction among them, but that his fatherly love and gentleness extend over all Christians and that his fatherly love and gentleness never cease.'

Following receipt of this letter, the King wished to learn more of the Khan of Eljigedei and of the Mongols. The envoys told him that Guyuk Khan's mother had been a Christian, a daughter of Prester John (Ong-Khan) and that about three years earlier he had had himself baptised with eighteen princes of his house. Eljigedei, who had sent them, had likewise been a Christian for several years, and the Great Khan had despatched him with a very powerful army to defend the Christian religion, to promote the liberation of the Christians and to fight against all their enemies. With all his heart he wished for friendship with the King of France, who, he heard, was coming to Cyprus. Finally, the envoys added that next year Eljigedei was going to besiege Baghdad, the seat of the Caliph. Rubruk undertook his journey to Mongolia, if not as ambassador, yet in the service of Louis IX. We may then definitely assume that he, as a man who stood close to the King, was equally acquainted with all these circumstances.

IN THE CAMP OF MUNGGE KHAN

At the beginning of May 1253 Rubruk left Europe. The journey involved no particular difficulty. But he had first to visit Sartakh and then his father Batu, and so arrived after long détours rather exhausted at the camp of the Great Khan, which was the actual goal of his journey.[16] His reception, and all that he found there, surpassed his expectations. The courageous friar must have been led to forget at once all the hardships of the journey and have felt that his efforts were richly rewarded. Guyuk Khan, who had been well disposed toward the Christians, had in the meantime died and Mungge Khan had stepped into his place. But the new Khan's attitude to the Christians was the same as his predecessor's. Rubruk tells with great enthusiasm how, eight days after the Feast of Epiphany (13th January 1254) Mungge visited the Nestorian church and his wife Qutoqtai Kadyn (Kutuktai Khatun), with her son Balta took part in the service and the Nestorian priests censed the Great Khan. On another occasion Mungge allowed a monk who had cured his wife to carry the Cross through the camp, to the great annoyance of the Mohammedans; and in princely fashion he presented a large sum of money to an Armenian priest. He regarded with great interest the Biblical books which Rubruk carried clasped to his breast; and when Rubruk visited the Khan's eldest son in his tent, the young man threw himself onto the ground, touching the earth with his forehead and worshipped the Cross. Rubruk must have found the information conveyed to him in Europe confirmed by these events and others like them, and we can well imagine that on receiving the summons from the Khan mentioned earlier he felt he was very near the goal of his missionary endeavour, and believed that the moment had come when the desires of the Pope, of his King and of all Christians would be fulfilled. But now at this audience he heard from the mouth of the Great Khan that he was no Christian but an adherent of shamanism. Furthermore he had to endure bitter reproaches directed against the greed for money and the contentious ways of the Christians. His disappointment was so great, that, as he says, in his consternation at the unambiguous answer that he received, he did not find occasion to present to him the Catholic faith. With resignation he writes in his report, 'After that I left his presence never again to approach him,' and adds as if with a sigh, 'Had I had the power to bring about signs and wonders like Moses, perhaps he would have humbled himself.'[17]

THE GOD OF THE SHAMANS

From the words of Mungge Khan we learn something fundamental about the shamans in general. In the first place that they believe in one single everlasting God. This supreme principle of shamanistic religion is confirmed by all medieval sources.

In Carpini's account of his journey likewise we find sentences that in phrasing and in meaning sound like those of Rubruk: 'They believe in one God, the creator of the visible and invisible world; they also believe that every good thing and all courts of punishment in this world originate from him; but they do not worship him with prayers or with songs of praise nor with any other kind of religious ceremony whatsoever.'[18]

We do not know how the Mongols imagined their God. Probably, as in all nature religions he was felt as a power that is active in men and in all created things. This is suggested by the words of Guyuk Khan, who in a letter to the Pope countered the reproach that the Mongols had invaded the Kingdom of the Macars (Hungarians) and Christians in these terms: 'In those kingdoms it is the everlasting God who has slain and destroyed. How could anyone even by God's order slay by his own might?'[19] What could men have done if God's power had not been at work in them? On their seals and documents the Mongols used the formula 'Tengri küchündür–by the power of God', which, after they had gone over to Islam, was stamped even on coins.

GOD IN HEAVEN, THE KHAN ON EARTH

The unshaken confidence of the Mongols in their Khan rested on their belief in a single God, who in their view had charged the ruler with converting his will into action. Thus the letter of Mungge to King Louis begins with the following words: 'It is the command of the everlasting God. In Heaven there is only one everlasting God, and on earth too there must be only one ruler, Chingis Khan.'[20] The supreme power of the Khan over the earth was indivisible, and his word was unassailable. Rubruk tells how it was proclaimed by the voice of heralds in the camp of the Great Khan: 'This is the command of Mungge Khan, and no man shall dare to say that God's command is different.'[21] The command of the Khans and the command of God were thus for the Mongols one and the same.

We learn further from the words of Mungge Khan that the adherents of the shamanistic religion possessed no Holy Scripture. The ideally conceived God of the monotheistic religions reveals himself in such a Scripture; the God of the Mongols is a power felt in the conditions of human existence, a reality which needs no Holy Scripture. The Mongols are not, as the Koran puts it, a People of the Book. They have no Scripture which lays upon them definite religious and moral obligations. 'In their religion,' says Ricold, 'they are distinguished from other peoples by not maintaining in lying fashion, as many other peoples do, that they had received their religion from God.'[22]

For Christians and Mohammedans, that is for adherents of a religion with a system formulated in fixed doctrines, this fact was unintelligible and often led to misunderstandings. The statements of many writers, that the Mongols had no religion or that they could not identify any religion among the Mongols, doubtless rest on such misunderstandings.

RELIGIOUS TOLERATION

This almost complete absence of dogma among the Mongols led to an explicit toleration of other religions. 'Because they have no definite law regarding worship (no binding rules for religion)', says Carpini, 'they have never yet, so far as we know, compelled anyone to deny his belief or his religion.'[23] The basis of this attitude was the regulation of Chingis Khan which guaranteed toleration to all religions and conferred on the clergy of various faiths one of the most important privileges of the Mongol nobility: exemption from taxes.

Everyone was permitted to adopt the form of religion which he considered right. While the rulers until the time of the Ilkhans were shamanists and Buddhists, the women of the royal family were mostly Christians. For example, the mother of Mungge Khan was a Christian, and so was Doqus Khatun, the wife of Hulagu. Abaqa's wife Maria was the natural daughter of Michael VII of Byzantium and likewise a member of the Christian Church. His second wife Qodai Khatun belonged to the Nestorian church and was of Mongol descent. In the religious upbringing of the children the mother played a great part, and two later Ilkhans, Oljaitu and probably Ahmed had received Christian baptism in their youth.

The people professed various religions. Before the rise of Chingis Khan the members of so important a tribe as the Kerait were Christians. After the founding of the Empire there could no longer be said to be any religious unity. The followers of various religions, Buddhists, Lamaists, Nestorians and Mohammedans enjoyed unlimited religious freedom, and in the imperial capital of Karakorum there were not only many Buddhist temples but mosques and churches.

The ruler behaved very correctly to the various religious bodies and in accordance with Chingis Khan's regulations treated them all alike. Rubruk tells how Mungge Khan, who was himself a shamanist, kept to his faith. But this circumstance did not prevent him from extending his protecting hand over the followers of other religions. He repeatedly recalled Chingis Khan's edict of toleration and confirmed the privilege of exemption from taxes for the clergy. Only the Jewish Rabbis were excluded from this, because Chingis Khan had not mentioned them. The attitude of Mungge Khan to Islam was no less friendly than his attitude to Christianity, already mentioned. Mungge visited mosques, gave money and building land for a medrese in Bukhara, and set up a supreme office for Muslim affairs under Imad-ed-Daula. That he was occasionally regarded both by Christians and by Mohammedans as a member of their faith is evidence for this attitude of his, aloof from sectional interests or above them.

There are few instances in Mongol history where we can speak of favour given to one religious community at the expense of another. Guyuk proclaimed a strong inclination toward the religion of the Saviour, so that he was at various times assumed to have personally adopted this faith. The Mohammedans had no easy time under his rule. But it cannot be assumed that the Christians planned the destruction of the Muslims, and even Mirkhond reports this with reserve.[24]

The hostility of the Ilkhans to Islam was more or less conditioned by politics. During the campaign of Hulagu it was the Caliphs and the Mameluke rulers who opposed the Mongols. The Mongols at that time saw the Mohammedans as enemies and the Christians as allies. After the fall of the Caliphate, therefore, great privileges were granted to the latter. Hulagu was known as their protector. He attended Christian services; his wife founded churches; the ringing of bells, forbidden in Islamic countries, was allowed, and the Christians were permitted merely to bow before the ruler instead of prostrating themselves. The Mohammedans, in contrast, felt the weight of the conqueror's arm. Mosques were closed, property was confiscated; the Christians marched into the town and sprinkled the Mohammedans with wine.[25] All this brought a reaction from the Mohammedans, and ended in bloody incidents. If the armies of Hulagu were greeted with jubilation by the Christians, the Mohammedans in 1277 received the Mameluke Sultan with joy in Kaisarieh, at which

20

Abaqa had the Mohammedan inhabitants of the town slaughtered without mercy.[26] But such events were conditioned by politics, and a few years later, in the time of Argun, who became a Buddhist, the vizier Sa'd-ed-Daula died for refusing to accept Mohammedans in the higher administration of the state.

Gazan was friendly to Islam and became a Muslim in 1295. Many Buddhist temples were plundered and relations with the Christians changed from good to bad. But as disturbances and excesses spread even more widely, Gazan felt himself obliged to order a check in the persecution. Plundering of churches was forbidden and he even went so far as to abolish the Christian poll-tax; Oljaitu, who continued his brother's policy, rejected the plan of turning a Christian church in Tabriz into a mosque.

By the conversion of Gazan to Islam the balance of religions in the Mongol Empire was decisively shifted, and it cannot be denied that in the sequel Islam won the victory in the struggle of faiths. If there had not been violent conflict at that time in Persia between the adherents of Sunna and Shia the most important sects of Islam, Islam would undoubtedly have become the religion of the state. The Shiites, the followers of Ali and his two sons Hasan and Husein who were murdered in Kerbela, disputed the right of succession to Mohammed. Under the Caliphs they had already been attacked, and for that reason under the Mongols they achieved a privileged position as compared with the Sunnites. Under the influence of the important Shiite scholar Nasir-ed-Din Tusi their position became stronger, and after the fall of the Ilkhan empire the Shiites gained the upper hand in Persia.

Their toleration in matters of religion, which had its foundations in the spirit of shamanism, shows also the great political acumen of the Mongols. For the conquered people 'it lightened the pressure of foreign rule and made the Government's task easier, since it brought about a moral order which could not be replaced by any police or organisation'.[27] Without this toleration it would probably not have been possible for the Mongols to maintain their rule for centuries in lands of ancient culture. Alexander's empire fell to pieces after his death.

IDOLATRY

Though the Mongols believed in one single God, shamanism is still different from the monotheistic religions that we know. The cult of the stars was widespread among them. They worshipped the sun, the moon and the stars. They saluted the sun by genuflecting three times facing southward. It was at sunrise and sunset that this simple ceremony took place. On important occasions great honour was shown to the sun. It is reported that after the election of Ogodai, Guyuk and all who took part went out of their tents to pray to the sun by genuflecting three times. The Mongols also worshipped fire and water, air and earth. Woods and caves, springs and mountains were sacred to them. When Chingis Khan was attacked by the Merkit tribe and with difficulty escaped capture, he offered thanks and sacrifice to the mountain Burkhan Khaldun as to a God.[28]

Gods of fertility protected their herds and the domestic god or *ongon* presided over the family's welfare. The Mongols believed in a close connection between living men and their long-dead ancestors. This belief brought about permanent ancestor-worship. Carpini relates how the Mongols dedicated to the dead horses that no man dared ride.[29] They worshipped Chingis Khan, founder of their people, like a god. In the camp of Batu Khan the Grand Duke Michael of Russia was commanded to bow southward before his image: his refusal cost him his life.[30]

We may ask at this point how among adherents of shamanism the belief in the highest God was compatible with star-cult, the worship of natural powers, and ancestor-cult. Were there in this case auxiliary gods beside the chief God or were these deities only different manifestations of the one highest God, who was worshipped in the form of the sun, the moon, and the powers of nature? If God was felt by the Mongols, as we have already hinted, to be an 'active power', the second possibility is the more likely. This assumption is confirmed by Max Müller, who in this connection writes as follows: 'Among the Samoyeds the name of the highest God was Jumala, that is, Heaven. Sometimes this highest God was imagined as the sun, on other occasions the same God was conceived as god of the sea, as lord of the air. By all these deities one and the same deity of Heaven is meant: Jumala.'[31]

All these gods were represented in visible form among the Mongols by idols in human shape. They were made of felt or clay and set up in various places. At the entrance of the tent on either side stood a figure; these according to Mongol belief protected the herds and guaranteed abundance of milk and young. Above the master's bed there was always an idol of felt, which they called the master's brother; a similar one, which was called the mistress's brother, hung by the head of the mistress of the house. Between these two protective idols, but a little higher, was one more tiny statue which served as protectress of the whole tent. When a child fell ill, an image was hung over his bed. In the middle of the camp there was also an idol which in their belief protected the warriors from danger.[32]

All these idols were served by the Mongols with offerings of food and drink. Marco Polo in his *Travels* described the ceremonies that were carried out on these occasions.[33] Before the meal the idol's mouth was smeared with a fat piece of meat and some of the broth in which the meal was prepared was tipped out at the door as a sacrifice for the other spirits. So too, when an animal was slaughtered, its heart was offered to the idol on a dish. As Rubruk describes it, the ceremony at the drink-offering was rather more elaborate.[34] After genuflecting three times to the four quarters of the sky, to the south in honour of fire, to the east in honour of air, to the west in honour of water, to the north in honour of dead ancestors, water was sprinkled from the goblet. At wine parties the Mongols are said to have cast the contents of the first goblet into the air and to have said 'That is the share which belongs to the sun.'

THE WHITE FEAST

On the 9th of May the Mongols celebrated a great feast, the so-called Spring Feast. All white mares in the herds were on this day rounded up and dedicated. This New Year Feast, or White Feast as it was also called, was celebrated in China in 1258 and 1259 under Mungge Khan. The celebration at the court of Kubilai Khan is described in great detail by Marco Polo.[35] According to his account there were in the stables about ten thousand stallions and mares, all as white as snow. No one was permitted to drink the milk of these mares except the royal family and the tribe of the Oirat, particularly favoured by Chingis Khan. 'So great was the respect shown to these horses, that no one dared to stand in their way or hinder them in their movements if they were browsing on the royal pastures.' It was a religious duty, ordained by the shamans, to scatter the milk of these mares 'into the wind' every year on the 28th of August 'as an offering to all the spirits and idols which they worship, in order to dispose them favourably and to secure their protection for the people, men, women, cattle, poultry, corn and other fruits of the earth'. His Majesty went on this important day to the place where he made the milk-offering with his own hand. The same is reported by the Persian historian

Wassaf.[36] At the accession of the Mongol-Chinese Emperor Kaishan (Chinese Wutsong) in the year 1307, drink offerings from more than seven hundred dedicated mares and seven thousand sheep were poured, so that the square in front of the *ordu* was like a milky way. These animals too were pure white and never touched by herdsmen: their flesh was not eaten and no one but the King could mount them.

THE SHAMANS

It was a condition of the nomad life that the Mongols should take their idols with them on fine covered waggons. These sacred waggons carried in the first place the ancestral images, which were worshipped like gods and which no one dared to touch. Anyone who stole from them was punished with death.[37] They were under the strict supervision of the priests, who were called shamans (Turkish *kam*) or soothsayers.

These soothsayers were mentioned by Mungge Khan in his audience: 'God gave the Christians Holy Scriptures,' he said, 'he has given us the soothsayers.' The High Priest (Beki) had his tent near the royal tent and directly in front of that of the Great Khan's first wife.[38] The shamans acted as spiritual counsellors. Prophesying the future seems to have been one of their principal duties. They foretold to the people eclipses of the sun and moon. When the eclipse came on, they caused drums and other instruments to be sounded and made a tremendous din in order to frighten away the evil spirits. After the eclipse a great festival of rejoicing was held. They prophesied which days were favourable and which unfavourable for the despatch of business, for military operations and the like. It was their task to determine the place where the horde should pitch camp, and when a child was born the family called the shamans to foretell its future. Prophecy by the stars was very widespread. But prophecy of the future was based on oracles which could take very various forms. In the sheeps'-bone oracle the shoulder blades of three sheep were thrown onto the fire, and length-wise cracks meant a favourable and crosswise ones an unfavourable conclusion to the enterprise that had been begun. In addition, there was an egg-oracle, a meat-oracle and a horse-oracle, the last determined by neighing.

There were also shamans who received answers from demons. These shamans believed that they were possessed by demons, and maintained that the demons told them everything that happened. Because of their extraordinary power they were feared and venerated. They communicated with the demons through the overhead opening in their tent roof. While the demons were being consulted the shamans danced with such frenzy that they finally collapsed as if dead. Others worked themselves up into such a violent state of ecstasy that, as Radloff reports, they had to be held down and firmly tied, which could be done only by the utmost efforts of several men. The bound shaman quivered and jerked for a long time after.

In all these actions the shaman kept his drum permanently with him, holding it in his hand and beating it vigorously with a monotonous rhythm. As Rubruk reports, hypnosis also was said to have been known to the Mongols for the purpose of prophecy.[39]

The shamans did not merely enquire of the spirits; they were also skilled in expelling evil spirits. By their conjurations they were able, so the Mongols were convinced, to set even the air in turmoil. Some maintained that they possessed a rain-stone with which they could make rain at any time. To hold off or to drive away storms was also one of the tasks of the weather-magicians. Marco Polo enthusiastically tells how the shamans, whom he calls astrologers and magicians, showed their skill in wondrous fashion at the Spring Feast. 'If the sky clouded over and it threatened to rain, they climbed onto the roof of the palace where the

Great Khan lived, held off the rain by their magical spells and conjured the storm away, so that even if there was rain, storm and thunder round about in the country, the palace remained unassailed by the elements.'[40]

In the view of the Mongols illnesses were mostly the result of conjuration, and so the shamans also functioned as physicians. The sick man's tent was marked by a spear stuck upright in the ground, or watchmen were posted in a wide circle round the tent to bar access to the patient because in some circumstances an evil spirit or a baneful wind could have made its way into the bed where he lay.[41] If any of the leading members of the court fell ill and it was feared that he would die, fifty or even more men would mount their horses and gallop round the great man's tent, swinging their spears right and left in order to keep off the angel of death.[42] If the angel of death would not be driven off and the sick man died, there were great funerary ceremonies. At the burial the deceased was presented with stuffs, draperies, food and mare's milk and an impaled and stuffed horse was set up on top of the grave. By the grave a funeral feast was held at which horse-meat was eaten. The remaining bones were burned after a three-day celebration in honour of the dead. The culmination of this ceremony was the purification of the tent. This procedure, though admittedly at a later date, is impressively portrayed by Radloff as follows:

> The shaman's highest accomplishment is the so-called purification of the tent. This is done on the fortieth day after the death of a member of the family. The purification is usually carried out with the special assistance of the Jajyk Kan, or water-god, and offerings are also made to him for this help. The purification is particularly important when several deaths have occurred in one family. For the Altaians believe that the soul of the deceased likes to linger for a time in the house and is unwilling to leave it alone, but often entices away other members of the family or of the household, or at least cattle, into the realm of the dead. Jajyk Kan is able, by bringing floods of water, to compel the return of the souls which have been partly enticed away and himself drive the soul of the dead down into the underworld. To a large extent this belief in the harmful influence of the soul of the deceased rests on the firm tie of kinship between living and dead kinsmen, which can be recognised as the foundation of shamanistic belief; it is also attributable in part to the many illnesses which work such fearful havoc among the Altaians, lacking as they are in any kind of medical assistance.
>
> In July 1860 I had the opportunity to be present in person at such a purification of the house, which took place by Lake Kengi. When, a little after sunset, I found myself in the tent where the ceremony was to take place there were about twenty persons assembled, kinsmen and neighbours. My host showed me to a place of honour close by the wall of the tent. He explained that his wife had died some weeks ago and that he had now called in a tried shaman from the Katunja to purify his house.
>
> When it began to grow dark the dull beats of the shaman's drum sounded at some distance from the tent. I stepped to the door of the tent and saw the shaman circling the tent with measured tread about a hundred paces away and singing his monotonous song in the same rhythm, from time to time beating hard on the drum. Gradually the shaman's circle grew narrower and narrower, until finally he walked close along the outside of the tent's wall and at last stepped through the door into the tent which was lit by a brightly burning fire. Now he approached the fire and held the drum above it facing in every direction in turn, so that the smoke blackened the inside and the outside of the hide of the shamanic drum. Then he sat down solemnly between the door and the fire and began his monotonous grating song, which he uttered in short abrupt tones. The song grew progressively softer and

softer and the blows struck from time to time on the drum gentler and gentler, until the song at last passed into a gentle whimpering moan and whisper.

Then the shaman rose carefully to his feet and walked stealthily round the tent, circling the fire, called the name of the deceased and turned his head to every side, just as if he were looking in the house for the woman whom he was calling. From time to time he spoke in a piping voice, mimicking the voice of the deceased, which implored him with a whimper to leave her with her family. She was afraid of the journey; it was so endlessly long that she could not accomplish it alone. She would so much like to stay with her children. Unmercifully the shaman drove her by the power of his drum, which before he came into the tent he had filled with many powerful spirits, from one corner of the tent to another. Only after long searching and driving did he succeed in catching the soul of the deceased between drum and *orbu* (drumstick) and thrust it with the drum against the ground. His song sounded now ever clearer and stronger, interrupted by the gentle whimpering of his prisoner.

Now the shaman turns the magic drum to face the ground, so that the beats sound dull and hollow as though they were pressing upward from the depths of the earth. The song too becomes more muffled and finally takes on a gurgling sound, for the shaman is leaving the tent and has set out on the way to the underworld, the realm of the dead. At the same time the singing grows ever softer and passes at last into a gentle whisper. With a violent beat he marks his eventual arrival in the realm of the dead. Now a conversation begins with the kin who died earlier and are in the realm of the dead and to whom the shaman is bringing the dead woman. They refuse to accept the new soul. The shaman tries to talk them over, begging and entreating; all in vain. Then he seizes the brandy bottle and gives the dead ones a drink of the water of life. They joyfully accept it, a lively jabber of all kinds of voices begins, which gradually take on a more and more babbling tone because the brandy is taking effect. The dead sing and cry out in joy and finally the shaman succeeds in smuggling the new soul in among them. Now the shaman's song grows progressively louder, because he has left the realm of the dead and is approaching the upper world again. When he reaches it he suddenly jumps up and is racked by violent convulsions. The song turns into a wild shriek; the shaman dances about the tent in frantic bounds until at last, bathed in sweat, he sinks unconscious to the ground.

The wild scene in the magic light cast by the fire made so powerful an impression on me that for a considerable time I followed the shaman with my eyes and quite forgot my surroundings. The Altaians too were overwhelmed; their pipes dropped to the ground and for a quarter of an hour stillness reigned without a sound.

The scene in the land of the dead is presented differently by different shamans in different circumstances. Often the attempt to smuggle in the dead does not succeed, often the soul escapes the shaman and returns to the tent; then he follows it and the scene begins again. If the shaman calls to his aid Jajyk Kan the water god, the merry scene of carousal in the realm of the dead is suddenly interrupted by the intrusion of waves. Then a general hubbub begins a wild scurrying to and fro. The shaman mimics the roar of the intruding waves. The dead scream for help, wailing and weeping. Now the cattle that the dead had driven off, or the souls of kin, are driven back home again. Many shamans are said to smear their faces with soot when they carry out this conjuration so that they may not be recognised by the dead in the underworld.'[43]

A purifying power was ascribed to fire. The tent of the deceased and all his possessions were subjected to purification by fire. Special purification was necessary for beasts, persons and objects if the tent was struck by lightning. Foreigners, particularly ambassadors, who came to the camp of the Great Khan had likewise to be purified; they were made to pass between two fires. Even the gifts that they presented were not touched so long as they had not been purified by fire.

Though the Mongols possessed no sacred book that imposed upon them definite commandments and prohibitions, they had none the less customs and traditions according to which certain actions had to be rigorously avoided. Thus in entering the palace it was regarded as an evil sign to touch the threshold. Marco Polo relates that at every door of the imperial palace there were two men of giant stature with staffs in their hands who kept watch to prevent people from touching the threshold with their feet and to force them to step over it. If anyone inadvertently committed this fault, the watchmen took away his clothes, or else they were instructed to deal him a number of blows.[44] The unwritten law also forbade anyone to cut up meat near a fire or to hold a dagger in the fire. It was likewise forbidden to strike horses with the bridle or to touch arrows with the whip, and other strictly proscribed acts were the killing of young birds, the emptying of milk or food on the ground and urination in an enclosed space.

Traces and remnants of these religious usages can be found in many countries of western Asia. No one any longer knows what they once meant; the medium in which they survive is widespread superstition, which to-day rests solely on a fear of ghosts.

STEPPE PEOPLES AND NOMADISM

'Good Mongols have a deep religious feeling; they think unceasingly of the other world and attach little importance to the things of this world. They live on earth as if they were not living there. They do not cultivate the soil and build no houses, they are as it were only strangers in transit, and the living feeling which pervades their innermost being, expresses itself in long journeys (pilgrimages).'[45]

With these fine words Huc sketches a picture of nomadism which is based rather on a romantic notion than on historical reality. The hard reality with which the Mongols always had to contend gave them little occasion for dreams of another world as they are represented here. In the *Secret History*, which provides the oldest account of this steppe people, we make the acquaintance of a series of nomad tribes, who, in contrast to the embellishments of later descriptions, were occupied with their herds and the game that they got from hunting, and had to carry on a continual struggle for existence.[46] Betrayal and attack, plundering, butchery and enslavement of enemies are the most important events that the author of the *Secret History* has to relate. Nothing here points to a belief in another world, to the miraculous stories and pious legends which appear so often in the later Chinese sources, and it appears that in the mental world of the Mongols the sense of the supernatural either was entirely absent or at least received very little recognition. This people, which, thanks to the spread and mobility of its mounted bands (with which heavily armed professional armies could not cope), founded the greatest empire in the history of the world, was possessed with one thought only, that God had conferred on it dominion over the earth. There is no evidence that they despised the treasures of this world and that the sense of property was in some way deficient among them. Booty from defeated enemies was by their conviction their lawful possession, of which a share was due to the ruler. Embezzlement of this share in the booty the Khan regarded as a curtailment of his royal prerogative. When at the capture of the town of Urgenj on the Aral Sea the princes Jochi, Chagadai and Ogodai divided the booty among themselves without setting apart a share for Chingis Khan, their father's anger was so great that he was mollified only by the mediation of his closest friends. Fighting for herds and pasture was common form among them. Hence pasturing grounds were assigned to tribes and, although they moved about, each tribe had its special grazing. 'The Mongols', says Rubruk, 'have divided the land from the Danube to the sunrise among themselves, and every chieftain, according as he has more or fewer people under him, knows the boundaries of his pasturing land, where his people may graze their cattle in summer and in winter, in spring and in autumn. In winter they wander off to warmer tracts in the south, in summer they move to cooler zones in the north.'[47]

ERECTION AND EQUIPMENT OF TENTS

The smallest social unit among the nomads to stay together in summer and in winter consisted of six to ten families and was called the *aul* (*agyl*, enclosure or hearth). They had round tent-like dwellings made of rods and thin staves. This light wooden frame was covered with black felt; the felt was often painted over with lime so that the tents shone white. The fireplace was in the middle of the inner space; above it was a round opening through which the smoke was carried off and the light came in. In front of the entrance a felt curtain was hung against wind and cold, but could be drawn up. Such curtains were adorned with embroidery representing vines and trees, birds and wild beasts.[48]

Small tents could be taken down in a very short time and put up again; they were carried on beasts of burden. The larger ones could not be taken to pieces. They had to be moved along on waggons which according to their size were drawn by one or more oxen.

A rich man could possess several hundred waggons of this kind. Batu Khan had twenty-six wives; each one had a large tent and each tent had two hundred waggons attached to it. One wife controlled twenty to thirty of these waggons. The waggons, drawn by oxen and camels, were harnessed one behind the other, and when a place on the route was reached which was difficult to negotiate, the waggons were unhitched from one another and manoeuvred in succession over the place.[49]

Ibn Battuta gives us his first impression of a great migratory camp in Kipchak in the following sentences: 'The imperial camp, which they called *ordu*, now approached. The whole outfit presented the appearance of a great town which was loaded onto waggons and kept in motion with all its inhabitants. One saw mosques, markets and the smoke that rose from the kitchens to the sky, for the Turks in fact cook as they travel, and one saw the *arabas* [waggons] drawn by horses, on which they drive.'[50]

When tent frames had been off-loaded from the waggons, the tents of the camp were set up in a definite order. In the middle, with its door facing toward the south, was the court encampment. Because the ground had to be unencumbered before and behind the court encampment, the tents of subjects extended eastward and westward, that is, on either side of the *ordu*, so that the whole looked like a village on the steppe. When Rubruk first saw the camp of Batu, the tents gave him the impression of a great town spread out in which people swarmed within a perimeter of three or four hours journey.[51]

The tents were put up with their doors facing south and the master's bed was set on the northern side. The women's place was always on the eastern side, that is, on the left of the master of the tent when he sat on his bed with his face to the south; the place for men was on the western side, that is, on his right.[52] The ruler's tent was made of specially fine material, usually linen. Because of its golden covering it was called the golden tent *(Altin ordu)*. Carpini graphically described such a tent, the one in which Batu held his magnificent court. The Khan sat in it surrounded by serried ranks of courtiers with one of his wives on a high golden throne; his brothers and sons and the high dignitaries were allowed to sit slightly lower down in the middle on a bench, while the rest of the people crouched behind them on the ground, with men on the right and women on the left.[53]

Though the Great Khans soon had large palaces built, on important occasions, such as elections, tents were used according to traditional custom. So Carpini reports that at the enthronement of Guyuk a great tent, made of white velvet, was pitched.[54] According to his estimate a good two thousand men could find room in it. The grandees gathered here and wore, on the first day of the imperial election, white, on the second day red, and on the third day blue ceremonial robes, while on the fourth day, which was the last day of the election, they were dressed in cloths fit for the finest canopies.

Marco Polo too mentions such tents *de luxe* in the eastern empire. Kubilai Khan was attended on his hunting expeditions by his whole family, by physicians, astronomers, falconers and all other court officials, and great tents of commensurate size were put up in which were various halls and chambers. The tent in which Marco Polo received an audience is said to have been so spacious that it could have contained a thousand men. The tent in which he and his attendants lived was somewhat smaller, but fell in no way short of it in the magnificence of its appointments. It was held up by gilded wooden pillars and covered on the outside with striped lion and leopard skins, on the inside with ermine and sable fur. The ropes with which the tent was secured were all of silk.[55]

RACIAL FEATURES OF THE MONGOLS

In 1239 Alberic describes the Tartars in the following manner according to the account of an eye-witness: 'They have a broad head, a short neck, a very broad chest, thick arms, short legs and possess a wonderfully great strength of body.'[56] In Carpini's description the wide distance between the slit-like eyes, the strongly developed cheek-bones, the small flat nose and the scanty growth of hair are emphasized.[57] We may compare with this the description by a later traveller, Radloff, who gives the following account of the people of the Altai who are very near to the Mongol type: 'With few exceptions they are of middle height, thick-set and broad-shouldered. The body is generally lean and very muscular; neither among the men nor among the women are there fat people. Hands and feet are small; the legs are usually bowed, their faces are wide and flat, the forehead is narrow, the cheek-bones are very prominent, the nose is flattish and far too small for the face, the mouth is large with thick lips and shows two rows of strong dazzlingly white teeth; bad teeth are found only among quite old people. The chin is usually pointed, the growth of beard very scanty even on the upper lip. The colour of the face is dark, hair and eyebrows are deep black, very tough and bristly.'[58]

The Mongols were distinguished by a peculiar haircut. On the crown of the head they had a shaven patch like priests, 'on the front of the head they leave a brush of hair that falls down as far as the eyebrows. In the same way they leave the hair growing on the corners and the back of the head. They plait these into pigtails and knot them as high as the ears.'[59]

The sources are unanimous in describing Mongol women as very fond of sport and skilled in riding and shooting but on the other hand definitely hideous and coarse. 'The women', says Radloff, 'lack any kind of elegance and the elastic walk which is peculiar to the female sex elsewhere.'[60] According to Rubruk they make themselves very ugly by painting their faces.[61] But this assertion is never confirmed; the fact is rather that they abominated face-paint. Chinese sources of the seventh century AD mention that the women of the Kirghiz tattoo themselves, but face-paint seems to have been unknown to them. It is told that it was first introduced at the court of Timur Lenk and that the women painted their faces with a white cosmetic to protect themselves against the sun.

DRESS

There was no essential difference between men's and women's clothing, except that the sack-like dress was longer for women than for men and reached down to the heels. But the women wore trousers under it. Clothes opened from top to bottom and were doubled over the breast; on the left side they were fastened with a single band, on the right with three bands.[62] The Tartars were distinguished from the Turks in fastening their clothes always to the right while the Turks fastened them to the left. Clothing material was imported from Baghdad, Persia and North China; the costly furs came from the forested regions of the north, from Russia, from Great Bulgaria on the Volga, from the lands of the Bashkirs and Kirghiz.[63]

The head-dress of the men consisted of a fur cap *(külah)*. It was only in Gazan's time that turbans were ordered to be worn. The women's head-dress was called *boqtaq (boghtak)*, and looked like an inverted boot. It was two feet high and ended square at the top like the capital of a pillar. Rich ladies wore this light head ornament of bark covered with costly silk and adorned on the top with the tail feathers of the wild drake, peacock's feathers, and precious stones. It was held firm with a hood, which had an opening for this purpose at the top, and was tied fast under the chin.

CHARACTERISTICS OF THE MONGOLS

Endurance of every kind of hardship seems to have been a general characteristic of the Mongols. According to the unanimous reports of travellers the secret of their unforeseen success lay in their power of resistance and their extraordinary frugality, shared by common soldier and prince alike.

'If they fast for a day or two without taking any food whatever, they are not seen to grow impatient but sing and play as if they had enjoyed the best of meals. In riding they can endure great cold and also on occasion support great heat; they are hardened and not sensitive to the effects of weather.'[64] Marco Polo later writes in the same tenor: 'Often they can, if necessary, hold out for a whole month in war without receiving any rations while they live on the milk of their mares, on game and on dried milk. Their horses too are content with grass from the field, so that they need not bring any supplies of barley, straw or oats for them.'[65] Similar remarks are found in Radloff. He writes that when in 1881 he wandered about by the sources of the Kemchik, 'neither cold nor heat, neither the long day's marches nor the discomforts of the journey over rocks, marshes and racing streams, neither hunger nor thirst seemed to make the least impression on his guides. Never was there a complaint or a word of reproach or a rebellious muttering, but always the same unruffled calm, the same cheerful mood, the same willing attitude.[66]

A further trait which the Franciscans report with admiration is their obedience: 'In the whole world neither among laymen nor among the brothers of the religious orders are there more obedient subjects than the Tartars: they show their masters more respect than other people and do not easily dare to lie to them.'[67]

Qasvini says the same: 'The Tartars practise such obedience to their kings that when a prince communicates to one of his governors the order to lay down his office and hand it over to another, he immediately complies with this order even when he is a year's journey distant from his master and has an army of fifty thousand cavalry under him.'[68] It seems that this trait, obedience to those in command, has been inherited down to the present day. Radloff writes of the Altaians, 'one trait of theirs is the high respect that they always show to age and their obedience toward every authority set over them. The commands of their own and of the Russian authorities are carried out punctually and without a murmur.'[69] Loyalty to the master, the legitimate ruler was respected even in their enemies. Thus those who betrayed their masters to Chingis Khan were beheaded.[70]

Lying was severely punished among them. In their view it was a crime which could in no circumstances be pardoned.[71] Likewise theft is said to have been unknown among them. Thus Ibn Battuta writes: 'There are horses in great numbers in Kipchak; they have no herdsmen or watchmen because of the strict laws of the Turks (Mongols) against theft.'[72] If cattle strayed, the finder either left them to their fate or brought them to the persons who were there for that very purpose. The owners of the strayed animals addressed their enquiries to these persons and got them back again without difficulty.

Though drunkenness was very widespread among the Mongols, it is said to have led very seldom to fighting, and one man showed the necessary respect for the other.[73] Travellers' reports both early and recent consistently praise the sense of unity among the Mongols. In this connection Radloff writes: 'Every poor man who attaches himself to the family of a rich man regards himself as a member of it... The whole people likewise forms a family whose members stand by one another in need. Everyone who steps into the tent is treated almost as a member of the family. If the family has a meal, he eats with them... you may give a Kalmuck what you will and he will share it with all present. They like sugar and bread better than anything. But if you give a piece of sugar to anyone present, he bites it into pieces so small that everyone present gets one.'[74]

They are said to have shown great respect for all women, particularly their own. The women appear to have been extraordinarily faithful to their husbands. Nothing is heard of any misconduct.

But all these admirable virtues of the Mongols are said to have been turned into their opposite in dealings with foreigners. Thus Carpini, who praises the Mongols as people who love the truth, says at the same time: 'they are the greatest liars in the world when they are dealing with other men (than Tartars) and scarcely a single word of truth is found in their mouths.'[75] Plundering of foreign goods was regarded as lawful. This people, so modest and peaceful at home, was extremely arrogant toward other men and looked with contempt on all others. They felt themselves the masters of the world and so extreme were they in their arrogance, according to Rubruk, 'that they were ashamed to be called Christians, even when they were, that they sought to extinguish the name of the kindred Tartars and put in its place their own name of Mongols, and that they thought that the whole world must conclude peace with them.'[76]

THE POSITION OF WOMEN

According to the Mongol law of marriage the wife was obtained by sale. Men enjoyed the right of unrestricted polygamy. Marriage was forbidden with a man's mother, his sister and his daughter, but not with his step-sister and other relatives. In spite of polygamy, Mongol women enjoyed greater freedom than did their Arab and Persian sisters. This freedom rested on a division of labour between men and women.

It was among the duties of women to drive waggons, to load tents onto waggons and off-load them again, to milk cows, to tan hides, to sew clothes, and to knit stockings, to make coverings of felt, etc., while men made bows and arrows, saddles, stirrups and bridles, carpentered and repaired tents and waggons and in time of peace occupied themselves with hunting and hawking. The women could ride like the men and many could handle a bow as well as men.[77]

The Mongols set a high value on descent and membership of a distinguished family, and for the choice of the chief wives of nobles only a few Mongol tribes which Chingis Khan had nominated were considered. Among these were the Oirat, the Naiman and the Christian Kerait, to whom Mungge's mother and Hulagu's wife Doqus Khatun, belonged.

The royal women could receive ambassadors and took part in various functions such as the choice of a ruler. The ruler's mother played a very important part in this. When, because of a calumny, Chingis Khan wished to put to death his brother Khasar, his mother took him by surprise. She arrived in wrath, climbed down from her waggon, herself untied Khasar's bound arms and set him free. According to the *Secret History*, which reports this affair, Chingis Khan was so terrified of his mother that he trembled.[78] In important events and decisions the ruler's wives were allowed to have their say. When Chingis Khan was setting forth on his western campaign, Queen Yesui proposed that he should designate one of his sons as his successor. To this proposal Chingis Khan is said to have made the following answer: 'Though Yesui is only a woman, her words are the rightest of all. None of you has ever before made such a suggestion. I too have forgotten to think of it, as if I were not bound some time to join my ancestors. I have been sleeping, as if I could never be overtaken by death.'[79] The Great Khan's choice fell on his third son, Ogodai, who was then elected Great Khan after his death.

HUNTING

Like all nomads, the Mongols were dependent on their herds. They lived chiefly on *kumys* (fermented milk) and meat.[80] Horses, cattle and sheep were bred in great numbers. But they were not sufficient for the demand, and in winter great state hunts had to be held, in which the high-born also took part. Chingis Khan's hunting ground lay in the neighbourhood of Almalik. Ogodai had a special hunting park laid out near Karakorum. By means of these hunts the feudal lords received the immediate yield of their appanages, and apart from that the troops were kept in training in peacetime.

We have full accounts of the hunts that were held in China. Marco Polo, himself a passionate hunter, gives a description of Kubilai Khan's hawking, in which ten thousand falconers with five thousand gerfalcons and many other hunting birds took part.[81] Gazan Khan limited the number of falcons at his court to a thousand. Later eight hundred falcons were kept at the Persian court, of which each had his own keeper. According to Radloff, hawking is still the favourite occupation of the rich Kirghiz.

In the great battues of Kubilai Khan, we learn from Marco Polo, twenty thousand hunters in red and blue uniforms took part. The hunting beasts included not only hounds, but leopards, lynxes and lions which were brought along in cages. 'It is a magnificent sight,' says Marco Polo enthusiastically, 'when the lion is let out and chases the quarry to see the wild greed and swiftness with which he catches it.'[82] With these hunting beasts were caught boars, wild bulls, asses, bears, deer, buck and other game. The eagles, which were trained to stoop on wolves, were so large and strong that no wolf could tear himself free from their claws.

This regulation requiring great hunts rested on the *yasa*, the lawbook of Chingis Khan. Under this the hunting of deer, roe, chamois, hares, wild asses and certain species of birds was banned from March to October, so that they could multiply.

THE MONGOL ARMY, WEAPONS AND STYLE OF WARFARE

The military miracle of the rise of the Mongol world-empire is explained by the superiority of the light and fast cavalry of the steppes over heavily armed professional armies. The structure of this army rested on the decimal system. The lowest unit consisted of ten men, the next above it of a hundred, and so on. Ten thousand men made up a division *(tümen)* under a divisional commander who was distinguished by a horse-tail banner *(tug)* and had flags and pennons of various kinds. The Mongol army consisted of several of these tümens, and on the field of battle was deployed in a right and left wing and a centre. The commanders of the army were subordinate to a supreme commander for the entire forces.

The nomination of the commanders was the ruler's affair, and in the selection the circles of the Mongol aristocracy were the first to be considered. The strict discipline of the Mongol army was proverbial. Disobedience seldom occurred; in war it was punished with death.

On the size of the Mongol army nothing definite can be said. Rashid-ed-Din speaks of a core of 130,000 men which in time of war was raised to ten times the number (up to 1,400,000 men). Under Ogodai 1,500,000 men in five armies are said to have been kept ready for battle.[83]

The Mongol army consisted mainly of cavalry. The infantry played a very unimportant part. For armour the soldiers wore chain mail, helmets, arm-guards and leg-guards, made of iron on leather. The horses too wore chain mail and their heads were protected by iron plates. The shield was leather or made of plaited osiers or twig. The bow-and-arrow was the chief weapon. The spear and the sword, which was slightly curved and pointed at the end, were used for close combat. For crossing rivers the Mongols had leather bags which they took into the field, and they had axes and tow-ropes for hauling their war machines.

When they marched to war they sent on an advance guard, which prepared the way for the main army. As soon as they saw the enemy, they rushed upon him. But if the enemy resisted, it did not lead to a proper battle, for they withdrew. In this way they sought to draw the enemy into an ambush.

The withdrawal could often last a whole day. In Kipchak they retreated before the Russians for nine days, and so too in Hungary from Pesth to the Sayo, only to take their exhausted enemy by surprise on ground favourable to themselves.[84] The battle began after they had surrounded the enemy on all sides. In battle they always left an alley open to their enemy for flight. As soon as the cohesion in the enemy ranks loosened and the enemy prepared to flee, the Mongols hunted them down from behind and killed more men in the flight than they had been able to hew down in the battle.[85]

Ruse was one of the indispensable methods of warfare. The great craft and cunning of the Mongols in war was emphasised by the Emperor Frederick II in his letter on the Mongol peril, in which he writes 'The Tartars are informed by their spies, whom they send out in all directions, of the quarrels and divisions in a country and know its weakest places which are least able to resist them. Though they are not enlightened by the light of the divine law, they are none the less in matters of war extremely sly and cunning.[86] Of the many stories of Mongol ruses in war we can mention only a few here. In war against the Christian Georgians they are said to have carried crosses before them in order to make the Georgians believe that they were

32

Christians and allies. When they conquered the town of Merv they had the call to prayer sounded to draw the inhabitants out of their secret hiding-places. Those who fell into this trap and appeared for divine service were killed. It is also reported that in the war against Hungary they wrought destruction on the inhabitants by means of a false proclamation from King Bela IV. When they surrounded their enemies they often used dummy men on horseback in order to make their number appear greater. They placed captives in front of them in battle, and these had first to take 'the impact of enemy weapons in all their destructiveness'.[87]

Carpini's assertion that the Mongols avoided close combat when this was at all possible is confirmed by Marco Polo. 'The Tartars never commit themselves to a regular hand to hand engagement but swarm round the enemy and discharge arrows at him. Then for a time they make as if they would flee, but in flight they turn about in the saddle and shoot violently and with all their might against the enemy... When by this means they have slain or wounded a great number of horses and foemen, they suddenly wheel about in a body and renew their attack in such perfect order and with such a loud cry that the enemy are quickly put to flight.'[88] This tactic of feigned flight, which was later used often by the Ottomans, was called by the Mongols the dog-fight, because dogs suddenly turn about in flight and make for the attacker.[89]

Their technique of warfare was unsurpassed not only in the open field but also in laying siege to fortresses. For this purpose they used a novel kind of ballista with which, according to Marco Polo, they could hurl stones up to 300 pounds in weight. They used mines, Greek fire—an invention of the Syro-Greek engineer Callinicus—and tried to flood the besieged town by damming up the river that flowed through it. By these means they reduced fortified towns which offered the most determined resistance, such as Samarkand in 1220 and Mardin in 1229. The conquest of these fortified places in civilized lands shows that they were able to achieve excellent results in siege-warfare and that they had no difficulty in handling the latest siege-engines. Certainly they were helped by capable workmen and engineers from civilized countries. Thus Hulagu was accompanied on his campaign in the west about 1253 by a staff of 1000 engineers from China. It is easy to see why the Mongols at war spared the workmen and artists in the enemy's camp: it was to place them in their own service. At the capture of Samarkand 30,000 workmen, and at the capture of Urgenj 100,000, were carried off; after the conquest of Nishapur, Kars and Erzerum it was the same. Because the Mongols, for fear of revolts, wished to have no enemies in their rear they treated the inhabitants of conquered towns and provinces with great brutality. Thus at the capture of Rayy, Merv, Nishapur and Baghdad respectively, 1,000,000; 1,300,000; 1,747,600 and 800,000 people are said to have perished.[90]

MONGOL LAW

The amazing military successes of the Mongols doubtless played a great part in the founding of the Empire. But at least equally important was the development in Mongol law, by which the members of this primitive tribe of nomads, rapidly reorganised, were able to maintain themselves as masters of the world in all conquered countries.

Before Chingis Khan the Mongols, who had no writing, had only a customary law. After the founding of the empire the need for a written record of legal rules became obvious. So, on the foundation of Mongol customary law and the collected decisions of Chingis Khan, the 'great law book', the *yasa*, was committed to writing in the Mongol language and the Uighur script. This work was kept with the imperial treasures, and at assemblies concerned with the law could be regarded as the ultimate source of law. The law-book contained regulations for dealing with foreign powers, for warfare, for the organisation of the army and establishment of a postal service, together with statements about taxation, inheritance and family relations.

The legislation of Chingis Khan was naturally directed entirely towards meeting current needs and had to be supplemented from time to time. This was done by collecting and setting in order as a completion and explanation of the law the sum of the legal decisions and pronouncements of his successors which formed the so-called *bilik* (Maxims). Important questions of law were also handled in the imperial assemblies. Not only Ogodai, Guyuk and Mungge, but also the Ilkhans based their actions on the *yasa*.

A change came with the conversion of Gazan and the Mongols to Islam in 1295. Thenceforward in practice the *yasa* receded more and more into the background. It had lost its validity through the growing importance of religious law.[91]

SCIENCE AND TECHNICAL STUDIES

Among the sciences promoted in the Mongol period historical writing occupied a special place. The first task of this science was to hand down to posterity the famous deeds of the great, but beyond this it was expected to provide encyclopaedic learning, in which the Mongols showed a lively interest. Among historical works of this kind the most important was Rashid-ed-Din's *World Chronicle*. Among the other sciences, those were preferred which were expected to have a beneficial influence on human life. They included medicine, which, with its study of healing herbs and Indian *yoga* exercises, combined ancient tradition with new knowledge, and astronomy, which in the medieval East could never be really separated from astrology. The large sums which are said to have been spent on the founding and equipment of the observatory in Maragha by Nasir-ed-Din Tusi (died in 1274) were granted by Hulagu and Abaqa without hesitation, though it was perfectly well known that the great astronomer was primarily concerned with scientific investigation of the heavens. Interest in fortification, in new engines of war and in weapons was very great among the Mongols; during his five years of instruction Gazan was taught mining as his principal subject, and Oljaitu as a young man is said to have been very well versed in military handicraft.

THE BUILDING OF TOWNS

The Mongols had certainly destroyed many ancient seats of culture, but they rebuilt them with great zeal. Thus towns like Bukhara, Herat, Termes, Gandsha, Nishapur, Baghdad, which during Chingis Khan's campaign had been almost levelled to the ground, were restored under the rule of his successors. Karakorum, originally founded by the Uighurs, developed when the Mongol Empire was formed into a flourishing royal capital. The new Ilkhan capital, Sultaniye, was created by the efforts of Arghun and Oljaitu, and although architects from all parts of the world took part in its building, it is nevertheless an important example of Mongol building in the west. In China there were also new foundations. These included in particular the city of Tai-du (Ta-tu means 'great court') which Kubilai had built next to Kambula (East Turkish, Khanbaligh—'Khan's town'). The river between the old and the new town is the Ta-thong-ho, a tributary of the Pei-ho. Both places are now known under the name Peking. Peking at the present day consists, as in the time of the Mongols, of two parts, rectangular in shape. One, which is almost a square, is the former Tai-du. The description which Marco Polo gives of the city agrees in essentials with the present appearance of the former Mongol quarter: 'The new town is laid out in the form of a square and has a perimeter of about twenty-four

Italian miles, so that each side is no more and no less than six miles long. It is surrounded with walls of earth, which at the bottom are about ten paces thick but gradually decrease toward the top, where the thickness amounts to no more than three paces. These walls are completely white. The whole plan is laid out with great regularity and the streets are therefore generally so straight that, if one comes in through one of the gates in the walls and looks straight ahead, one sees the opposite gate on the other side of the town. Along the streets on both sides are set booths and emporia of the most varied kinds. All pieces of ground inside the town on which dwelling houses are built have the form of a rectangle and lie next to one another in a straight line, and every plot has sufficient room for buildings with attached courts and gardens... In this fashion the whole town is divided into rectangles, so that it is like a chessboard and its plan shows an indescribable regularity and beauty. The wall round the town has twelve gates, three on each of the four sides, and over each gate and in every section of wall stands a graceful building, so that on every side there are five such buildings. They contain large rooms in which the town's armouries are established and every gate is guarded by a thousand men... In the centre of the town there hangs on a building a great bell which is struck every night and after the third stroke no one may any more be seen on the streets.'[92]

Beyond each gate lay a suburb which was so extensive that it reached on either side as far as the suburb by the next gate, and was linked with it, so that the number of inhabitants in these suburbs surpassed that in the inner town. Here were many shops and caravanserais in which the merchants who came from different lands could find accommodation; one house was reserved for the Lombards, another for the Germans and a third for the French. The number of prostitutes, if those in the new town and in the suburbs of the old town are counted together, reached 25,000 according to Marco Polo.[93]

PALACES, PLEASURE-CASTLES, PARKS AND MARVELS

In Tai-du some of the imperial palaces and great public buildings of the Mongol period may still be seen. The Great Khan usually resided during the winter months in the great city of Kambalu. The palace of the Great Khan is described by Rashid-ed-Din, a contemporary of Marco Polo, in the following terms: 'The pillars and facing-tiles of the palace are all made of hewn stone or marble and present a magnificent sight. Four walls surround and protect it. The distance from one wall to the next is so great that an arrow shot with great force just carries across them. The outer court is reserved for the palace guard, the next one for the princes who gather there every morning, the third is occupied by the great dignitaries of the court and the fourth by persons who belong to the ruler's immediate entourage...'[94]

The imperial armouries were housed in eight great buildings and each building contained a particular kind of weapon. 'Thus for example, the reins, saddles, stirrups and other gear that belongs to the equipment of the cavalry occupy one store house, the bows, strings, quivers, arrows and other material required for archery are to be found in another; mail, armour, and leather fighting equipment in a third. The imperial wardrobe is accommodated in eight further large buildings. In the back of the main palace are large rooms in which the Emperor's gold and silver, worked jewels and pearls and all gold and silver vessels are kept.'

Near the palace was an artificial hill, covered with the 'most beautiful evergreen trees' which earned it the name of the green mountain. These choice trees were dug up at the Emperor's behest, roots and all and no matter how large they were, in widely separated regions and brought hither by elephants for transplanting. Near-by there is said to have been also an ornamental lake, populated with swans and other waterfowl, which was created by digging a deep trough, the earth from which was used to build the hill.

The marble palace of Kubilai Khan in the town of Xandu (*Shang-tu* means Palace of the Ruler and was the name of the summer palace of the Yüan in Kai-ping-fu) once aroused wonder too because of its magnificent planning. The place was renowned for its soft air and healing springs. We have already described the royal stables there in detail. In the great park lush and beautiful meadows had been laid out, watered by many streams. There was also a great game-reserve harbouring wild animals of all kinds. In the midst of these gardens in a 'pleasant grove' Kubilai had a royal pleasure-castle built resting on beautiful gilded and painted pillars and set up in bamboo. 'The whole was built with such skill,' says Marco Polo, 'that all its parts could be dismantled, carried off and re-erected wherever it pleased His Majesty.'[95]

When Rubruk visited the royal palace at Karakorum, he admired at its entrance an artificial fountain which he describes very fully. The fountain took the form of a great tree of silver. The four lions by its root, likewise of silver, spewed out white mare's milk. Four golden snakes coiled round the trunk right up to the top, and from their mouths flowed four different drinks (wine, karakumys, honey and rice beer) into vessels standing beneath them. High above the tree stood an angel with a trumpet in his hand, and beneath the tree another space was hollowed in which a man could be kept concealed. When the chief cupbearer called out, this man had to make wind with bellows to cause the trumpet to sound. At this sign servants began to pour drinks into the fountain from the storechamber outside the palace. The drinks which then flowed out of the snakes' mouths were carried by the cupbearers into the royal palace.[96]

This fountain, which was made on Mungge Khan's order by the French goldsmith Guillaume Bouchier, was no doubt modelled on similar works of art in western courts. There are reports of a gold plane tree at the court of Darius I, and the throne of Solomon with its golden tree had a legendary fame in the Middle Ages. On this was modelled a similar work at the court of the Caliph Muktadir in Baghdad. The tree at the court of Muktadir is said to have been of silver and free-standing. Its gilt branches and leaves moved to and fro at the lightest puff of wind, and gilded and silvered birds flew and twittered in a great variety of tones. At the Mongol court of Sultaniye too there is said to have been a golden tree with pipes inside it, from which poured all kinds of drinks. The fountain which Rubruk describes must have been very like this.

Though the Mongols were heirs to a great tradition of painting, we learn very little of the activity of painters at the Mongol court. We have detailed descriptions of the equipment of tents. The abundant motifs taken from the world of animals and plants for the adornment of tents had the character of hatchwork or appliqué work made of leather or felt. But it is impossible to get any idea of Mongol painting from this decoration. We read in Carpini that all round the great electoral tent was a fence of boards or panels painted with various pictures. What these pictures represented and how they were painted is not mentioned.[97]

In the countries occupied by the Mongols the Chinese were renowned as the most skilful masters in the world in all the products of human aptitude. Their talent for painting was proverbial in the east. Ibn Battuta relates how he visited the imperial palace in Peking with one of his companions; when he passed through the painters' market in the evening on his way back, he saw his own picture and that of his companion painted on paper and glued to the wall. This is said to have been done by order of the Emperor.

By his order a picture was made of everyone who passed through his country. If a foreigner should take flight because of a crime that he had committed, his picture was sent into all the provinces, and on its evidence he could be found and arrested.

MONGOL PAINTING

THE MONGOLS IN THE WEST

The position of the Mongols was not the same in all the lands that they occupied. The Chinese were at that time the most cultured people on earth and felt until the end that the Mongols were barbarians. All traces of them were wiped out as soon as they left the country in 1367. In Kipchak Russia the population was, in contrast to the Chinese, quite primitive: here the Mongol domination lasted longer. One would have expected that the Mongols would make a deeper impression on the life of the people and that they would have left some permanent traces there. But the deep religious feeling of the people worked against the Mongols, and here too they could exercise no permanent influence. In the west, that is to say in Iran and neighbouring lands, the case was different. The Mongols appeared here as the bearers of a foreign culture. When they went over to Islam, they were no longer felt by the native population to be foreign conquerors as in the eastern empire of Yuan China or in the territories of the Golden Horde. Thanks to this rapprochement, an independent culture could arise in the west, in which the east's share was very great and sometimes even surpassed that of the west. Thus, if we can speak of any flowering of culture brought about by the Mongols, the Near East only comes into question.

ISLAMIC BOOK-PAINTING OF THE PRE-MONGOL PERIOD

Though painting of the pre-Mongol period in the Near East is called the Baghdad School, it is not to be localized simply in the caliphal seat of the Abbasids, for its monuments appear not only in Iraq but also in Greater Syria, Egypt and far beyond in regions between Spain and Morocco in the west and the Iranian plateau in the east. In this wide territory were many nations of different languages. The essential bond between them was the religion of Islam, and this circumstance carried more weight than all their national peculiarities. In the rise of the Baghdad School the influences of Byzantium, of Manichee-Uighur and Nestorian Christian circles played a part which must not be underestimated. But they all went into the crucible of Islam. Thus in the painting of the Baghdad School we are dealing with a line of artistic development which, though a mixed product of many and often opposing influences, still has, as a creation of Islamic civilization, a completely unified character and style.

In Islamic belief Allah, in contrast to the Christian God, is hidden in a transcendent world which no human eye can penetrate. The conception of a 'hidden God' necessarily led to a strict prohibition against depicting him.[98] In practice this prohibition caused artists in general to feel a pious reluctance to touch religious themes. Hence Islam knew no religious painting like that of the Christian countries of the west. The way to truth led through the Koran, holy scripture. Only a very subordinate role was allotted to art, and on the edge of the spiritual world of Islam a form of painting arose which served more or less as entertainment.

The painting of the Baghdad School developed in this direction, though it was not free from religious and moralising tendencies. For choice of themes the literature of entertainment, which at this time was extremely popular in circles outside the court, proved an inexhaustible source. Among the finest examples of this kind of literature are *Kalila and Dimna (Kalila wa Dimna)* and the *Makamas* of Hariri. The first of these is a book of fables which has animals for heroes and is named after two jackals, the principal characters. Behind this peculiar work was an ancient collection of Indian animal fables which were ascribed to a wise Brahmin named Bidpai. The Indian book of fables was conceived as a 'mirror for princes' and in the Islamic world was known in Arabic and Persian versions; it was illustrated from the early Islamic period onward.[99]

The '*Makamas*' *(Maqamat)* of Hariri were particularly prized by cultured people because of the brilliant literary style in which they were cast. But the broad masses enjoyed them too, particularly the hero Abu Zayd, who elbows his way through life as an unscrupulous vagabond and delights the people with his tricks. According to Ettinghausen he is the literary counterpart of the rather later 'robbers' *(ayyarun)* 'who in the great cities of the Muslim world, especially Baghdad, in the middle of the twelfth century, tried to exercise a levelling form of social justice by equalizing property and counteracting the efforts of the authorities to maintain order.'[100] We do not know at what date the *Makama* illustrations first appeared. Similar themes are often used in the east in popular puppet-shows and shadow-shows, and we may assume that various *Makama* manuscripts were very early adorned with pictures. The oldest known versions of the work come from the first half of the thirteenth century. They are copiously illustrated.[101]

The illustrations to the *Makamas* and to *Kalila and Dimna* are among the most important paintings that were ever produced by the Baghdad School. Apart from these, we should mention the illustrations to the scientific books. In this group we are concerned with philosophical, historical, medical and astronomical works translated from Greek into Arabic. Among them the *Book of Herbs* by Dioscorides, the *Book of Antidotes to Poisons* by pseudo-Galen, and various philosophical aphorisms of the Greek sages were particularly well known in scientific circles.[102] Since, as in the Byzantine originals, a supply of direct illustrations was thought necessary for the understanding of the subjects treated, these books too were illustrated. The illustrations were primarily of value as material for demonstration, and although they will always charm by virtue of their artistic quality, they cannot, except in a remote sense, be understood as paintings expressing the spirit of the Baghdad School.

Not only the themes but also the manner of representation in the Baghdad School were very largely determined by the religion of Islam. In the Mohammedan's view the world in which we live is a world of appearance, subject to mutability. Was such a world of appearance and illusion worth representing in art at all? Two ways of meeting this challenge were open to the artist: either he took refuge in the realm of fantasy or he changed the actual world into an imaginary one, for until this was done it could not in his eyes have any representational value. In the first case art became an abstract plan of lines and forms; this was the origin of the arabesque, remote from nature. The second line of approach resulted in the miniature. The dissolving of the material element in nature was certainly the most striking feature of this art, which thereby came near to being a shadow-play. Thus the shapes which make up the scenery in painting of the Baghdad School are often as flat as those of the movable scenes in a shadow-play, and the figures, set in relation to one another with characteristic poses and gestures, appear in their fixed outlines as figures of silhouette, glittering with colour and transparent, which likewise recall the figures of a shadow-play.

The drive for abstraction is so much a mark of Islamic art that in the figures that they copied from Byzantine originals the illustrators of the Baghdad School remodelled the naturalistically rendered folds of dress into the ornamentation called 'frilled folds'.[103] The manner of representation in Islamic miniatures is remote from all naturalistic methods of painting. It shows no copies of nature, but symbolizes ideal forms, which, in their abstract and schematic rendering, are but symbols of the transitory world and bear witness to the reality of the unique existent Being, namely Allah.

In the development of Islamic miniature painting we can distinguish a realistic trend as well as an idealising one. In the idealising vein, art leads us beyond all the blemishes of this world away into gardens of paradise where dream-princes live and move. The finest example of this trend is provided by the Persian miniatures of the sixteenth century. The art of the Baghdad School, on the other hand, is realistic; its style of representation, as we see in the *Makama* illustrations, far from beautifying its subject, often verges on caricature, in which human folly is treated with humour but sometimes subjected unmercifully to ridicule.[104]

THE EASTERN TRADITIONS OF FIGURE-PAINTING IN THE WEST AND THE ORIGIN OF THE MONGOL STYLE

With the Mongol invasion the eastern traditions of figure-painting reached the West. The influence of the east is noticeable here and there in the art of Mesopotamian lands even before the invasion.

But, while up to this moment we saw no more than a very long-standing cultural relation between east and west, now eastern influence increased to such a degree that the art of the Near East fell back entirely into the wake of Far Eastern art. Everywhere Far Eastern forms of imagery made their appearance: elements of landscape such as clouds, water and mountains, a great variety of animals, the dragon, the simurgh and other fabulous creatures made their way as an eastern repertory of images from the homeland of the Mongols to the west and were incorporated into the miniature-painting of the Islamic world. This change of orientation extended the range of themes for representation in an unexpected manner. In the east the pictorial figure was not a medium for entertainment as it was in the Islamic world. Among the new achievements of the Mongol era were landscape-painting and the pictorial embodiment of epic historical and religious themes. The enrichment of iconography went hand in hand with a new approach to art that bore the stamp of the late antique period of the Central and East Asian cultures, and required a new attitude to the world, which the Islamic culture of the pre-Mongol period would have found inconceivable. The work of this period is imbued with a spirit quite different from that which invests Islamic book-illustration. We are still concerned mainly with illustrations to manuscripts, it is true, but they now have something of the monumental grandeur we find in the wall paintings of East Turkestan rather than in the miniature paintings of the pre-Mongol period. The art of the Mongol period is given over to an effort to show sculptural and spatial values which were not at all in the mind of the Baghdad School. The pictures reproduced in this book show in their style an earthiness and a closeness to nature which often recall the works of the Early Renaissance. The new style touches frontiers where we may speak, though with reserve, of a discovery of nature. In the realistic spirit of the Mongol period the east seems to have had an intimation of the way, though it did not find it, to a Renaissance of its own. But the succeeding period, beginning with the Timurid style, fails to maintain any organic development of the artistic effort of the fourteenth century which held so much promise. Rather it seems that these efforts came to grief in the violent reaction which they provoked in religious circles. With the Mongols the art of the Near East reaches the threshold of the modern Age: but thenceforward it loses itself more and more in the Arabo-Persian cul-de-sac, where so many gifted artists exhausted themselves beyond escape in sterile over-refinements and in constructing artificial paradises.

HEROIC LOVE
Illustrations to the manuscript of the poem Warqa and Gulshah

Among the known illustrated manuscripts of the Near East, the first work that allows us to speak of a Mongol influence is the manuscript of the poem *Warqa and Gulshah* which originated in the Seljuk period. Warqa and Gulshah are the names of a pair of lovers whose story, like those of Leyla and Mejnun, Kerem and Asli, Yusuf and Zuleika, is still alive in Islamic lands. The manuscript, discovered not long ago in the Topkapu Museum at Istanbul, contains seventy perfectly preserved miniatures in broad format. The poem is based on a legend that relates to the Arabian tribes of Mohammed's time. It has spread through the east since the seventh century, and we even find it again, no doubt coming by way of Spain, in medieval French literature under the name *Floire et Blancheflor*. It is entirely possible that the Topkapu manuscript, which, as noted in its introduction, was a present to the Sultan Mahmud of Ghaznah (998–1030), is the first

1 Warqa and Gulshah

40

سمبرامذودست ورقه کشاد | سوک لشکرخویش رفتند شاد

2 Duel

translation of *Warqa and Gulshah* into Persian. But the miniatures must, to judge by features of style that allow only one interpretation, have been produced in the first half of the thirteenth century, probably in Shiraz. Thus our manuscript will be a later copy of the original text.

The form of love in Warqa and Gulshah is in contrast to the Platonic, the epic form which goes back to early Islamic and even to pre-Islamic poetry. In Platonic love, as it is described in the *Symposium*, the lovers seek one another in vain. The motive force is unsatisfied longing; it gives the lovers occasion to express their feelings in exaggerated forms, they entreat and implore, groan and sigh, until they grow thin with the agonies of love and waste away. Because in the social framework of Islam the life of the woman is separate from that of the man, the 'Platonic love' that was taken from the Greek novel could be widely propagated in Islamic poetry: it even provided the poet with the only legitimate form in which he could sing the praises of love. It is different in *Warqa and Gulshah*. Here the lovers not only suffer but even fight for their happiness. Melancholy scenes are certainly not lacking, but they are confined to a few pictures, and in the surviving miniatures there are even violent scenes of battle between the Arab tribes in which both lovers appear as principal characters. It is noticeable that the woman's part in these episodes is no less important than the man's. Gulshah is always at Warqa's side and fights along with him: in one of the miniatures reproduced here 2 we see her, fully armed and mounted on her charger, killing the chief of her lover's rivals in open fight.

Like other miniatures, those of Warqa and Gulshah lead us into the world of imaginary forms that belongs to the Islamic miniature, in which truth to nature, relieved of the weight of matter, turns into the abstract forms of an ornamental pattern. Here there is no close affinity in style with the miniatures of the Baghdad School. The ornamental plant-motifs might have been extracted from Dioscorides, and the animal drawings could derive from *Kalila and Dimna*. This art is indifferent to all individual variations of natural forms. In the figures, with their round faces and four plaits, we recognize the Seljuk-Mongol type, which even in the pair 1 of lovers shows none of the traits that belong to portraiture. The rendering of the horses is the only exception. Movement is represented by markedly turning the head and body in divers ways, in which the strong 2

41

influence of a naturalistic tradition of illustration native to the Far East is to be recognized. Yet elsewhere among the miniatures we come again upon the symbolic language of the pre-Mongol period. One or two plants represent a garden, long sleeves are a sign of mourning, raised arms a symbol of panic, and a naked upper body indicates a slave. In the battle-scenes the painter does not delineate the actual movements of his figures: rather he sets before us images of movement, all identical, in order to convey the concept of battle. A rider beside a tent means that people are setting out on an expedition. The forms are simply signs, the painting a form of writing. The instructed person can without difficulty decipher this picture-writing in detail and interpret the scenes represented. To make that easier, the illustrator adds explanations in writing to individual pictures. But the labelling of the figures with their names does not come from the hand of the painter; it was added later.

Though our miniatures might be classified, both by their date of origin and by their abstract style, among works of the pre-Mongol period, yet the manner of their pictorial narrative already indicates some Mongol influence. The miniatures of the manuscript follow fairly closely the story of the two lovers. They become acquainted at school, they have to part, and are united by the Prophet only after their death. The whole story is broken up into single groups of scenes which, like the 'cantos' of epic poetry, tell of love and its sorrows, of manly courage and loyalty. A distinctive feature of the narrative presentation is the well-thought-out sequence of the pictures, in which preparatory and retarding elements are brought into play and decisive turning-points clearly marked. The culminations are reached after rapid successions of scenes of furious combat, each pressing close upon the last, and the action often breaks off suddenly with the death of two opponents. This is narrative in pictures. Thus the point is not to illustrate single episodes, which, each of more or less equal importance, might be threaded like beads on a string. For this kind of additive juxta-position the Baghdad School provides enough examples.[105] In the miniatures of our manuscript, on the contrary, the successive phases of a narrative are rendered running through the entire work in a skilfully planned strip-composition. We have no models for such a method of presentation in the painting of the Near East. The pictorial art of narration points rather to Central Asia for its origin. In fact the artists of East Turkestan adorned their cave-sanctuaries as early as the seventh century with wall-paintings which showed in friezes one above another the stories of Buddha's life *(avadana)* and of the events leading up to his birth *(jataka)*, legends and popular tradition by which, following the inner logic of events, they tried to make the deepest possible impression on the beholder.[106] Pictures in the Uighur kingdom had all the power and significance of words, and painting was here, to judge by the finds from Turfan which have come down to us, at least equal in status to religious texts. It was otherwise in the Near East. There the picture was so much thrust into the background by the word that the powers of expression of the one cannot be measured by those of the other. Narrative was the business of language and not of pictures. The texts of illustrated works were mostly anecdotes, in which the point was more important than the narrative. So in the *Makama* texts language celebrated its triumph in a pyrotechnic display of metaphors, ingenious jokes and allusions, while the illustrator's task was no more than to characterise as accurately as possible the chief figures of individual *Makamas*, who gave occasion for these verbal feats, through gesture, facial mien and costume. Faced with subjects that required an epic form of presentation the picture-language of Baghdad was dumb. The pre-Mongol period has a series of literary works in which there is narrative, but these were not illustrated. Among the widespread love-stories of Islamic poetry *Warqa and Gulshah* was certainly not the first to be illustrated, but it is the first work in which the illustrator tries to render the whole story in pictures as well.[107] The *Shahname (Book of Kings)* of Firdausi had to wait nearly three hundred years before it was illustrated for the first time. Only under the influence of the Mongol conquerors, when the epic painting of the Far East began to have its effect in Near Eastern lands too, did artists venture, if hesitantly, into this world, eventually to fall all the more compulsively and permanently under its spell.

HEROIC EPIC
Illustrations to Firdausi's Shahname

The *Book of Kings*, the *Iliad* of the Persians, was written at the beginning of the eleventh century. Firdausi worked at it for thirty years and dedicated it to Sultan Mahmud of Ghaznah, the 'founder of Persian poetry and higher culture', as Goethe apostrophized him. In this epic of 60,000 double stanzas, history and legend, official sources and popular tradition have been inseparably compounded and turned into saga. The poet celebrates in his work three different groups of themes all three of which 'interpenetrate as acts of a tremendous drama of the nations and of which the real hero is Persia itself'.[108] The centre of gravity for the whole poem lies without a doubt in the Book of the Heroes of old Iran, while the book on the history of the Sassanids and the saga of Iskandar (that is, Alexander the Great), who after his victorious campaign through Asia was to become a legendary figure in the imagination of orientals, remain subordinate to the heroic saga of Iran.

3   Isfandiyar's Fight with the Dragon

4 Isfandiyar's Fight with the Simurgh

Of the illustrated copies of the *Book of Kings* that survive and are known to us, the earliest date from the beginning of the fourteenth century. To these belong the miniatures illustrated in this book, which are taken from two manuscripts of the *Shahname*. One of them is in the possession of the Saray Library in Istanbul (Hazine 1479); it is completely preserved, both illustrations and manuscript. Its date of origin as given by the colophon of the work is 1330. The text of the other *Book of Kings* is unfortunately lost and the illustrations have reached us only in part. They are in a Saray album that once belonged to the former Prussian State Library (Diez A. Fol. 71), but is now stored at Tübingen; the peculiarities of style suggests that they were painted in Shiraz at the beginning of the fourteenth century.[109]

A fixed tradition for illustrating the *Shahname* had not at this time been established, and so we may assume the masters who produced our miniatures had to depend more or less on their own powers of 'inventing' pictures. Strong stimulation from the poem itself played an important part; the main task of the artist consisted in transmuting the poetic original into pictorial form. Since in the miniatures before us we are dealing with one of the earliest bodies of illustrations to the *Book of Kings*, we are justifiably astonished, in

44

looking at individual pages, at the masterly character of the pictorial narration, which is in no way inferior to the poetical in the formal arrangement of the scenes. Pictures and words in the miniatures are in fact so thoroughly attuned to one another that the relationship between them is always clear. We recognize without an effort Siyawush leaping through the funeral pyre, Isfandiyar battling against fabulous beasts, the four *7* loyal followers of Kai Khusrau meeting their death in the mountains, King Khusrau appearing before the *3–5* castle of the fair Shirin, who greets him from the fortress, or Bahram Gur on his hunt in the mountains making his master-shot and pinning the foot of a fleeing gazelle to its ear with his arrow.

In the *Shahname* the poet's imagination moves in territories where the real and the fantastic interpenetrate. The heroes of the *Book of Kings* are giants equipped with extraordinary powers, who measure themselves in their miraculous feats against monsters and demons. The monstrous and fantastic quality of the poetic vision is transferred to the pictures. The heroic figures of the *Book of Kings* in the Saray Library in fact lack every kind of individual characterization. They are distinguished from one another, not by such things

5   The Four Faithful Companions of Kai Khusrau

45

as traits which can be rendered in a portrait, but simply by a few abstract marks which are repeated like stereotypes. They thus become abstract pictorial symbols whose interpretation is left to the imagination and which thereby exert an unsuspected power of suggestion over the beholder. Even the world in which these figures move is as unreal as it could well be. The landscape of the miniatures is not modelled on any region on earth; it is a mythical realm, unbounded and not to be comprehended, which belongs to the *Shahname* alone. With reality as we know it, this world no longer has any connection, or at the most only superficial contacts. It is peopled by fabulous beings and mythical beasts such as Simurgh and the dragon, the Div Avkan and the Peris, creations of fantasy in which the forms of nature are glimpsed like vague recollections.

The language of forms in the *Shahname* illustrations of the Saray Library is a symbolical language which bears a close relation to ornament. Thus the landscape here consists of a few abstractly rendered plant motifs or of schematically indicated mountain peaks painted in improbable colours and producing the effect of an ornament. The shapes which the fabulous beasts assume are among the *motifs de luxe* of this style of ornamentation; but even the figures of the heroes are variations of a main decorative motif, among whose elements are the stylized floral pattern of the clothing, the interlace-work of the chain mail or the face set rigidly in the fashion of a mask. The surprising thing is that in spite of this clearly discernible tendency to an ornamental remodelling of the whole, the picture itself is not reduced to a mere piece of decoration. The 'meaning' of the picture is dominant in every case and the signs composing it never cease to 'signify' something. Their very closeness to ornament allows of a fullness of meaning which goes far beyond a naturalistically rendered scene or background; it is the highest concentration of everything set forth in the original text.

The *Shahname* illustrations from the Berlin collection are painted with a naturalism which is remarkable for this period. In *The Birth of Rustam* we have a particularly convincing example. The birth-scene was far from uncommon as a theme for representation in Near Eastern art. In the *Shefer-Hariri* of the year 1237

6   The Birth of Rustam

46

7 Prince Siyawush's Ordeal by Fire

(Paris: Bibliothèque Nationale, Arab MS 5847, Folio 122 verso) we find a similar scene in which the protagonist is shown with an almost unrelenting realism.[110] There is, however, a difference in the method of representation. The page of the *Shefer-Hariri* is executed in the abstract style of the pre-Mongol period. The rendering of the miniature here reproduced is on the other hand naturalistic. The uncovered parts of the woman lying in labour are delineated in a very sculptural manner of half-tones and soft lines, and one notices that the illustrator knows the structure of the human body accurately.

Even the 'frilled folds' of the *Shefer-Hariri* are here replaced by naturalistic folds in the dress, whose curves are well adapted to the anatomy of the body. A kind of aquarelle-like shading of the colours gives support to the linear modelling, so that even the stylistically-rendered formation of the ground gains a palpable solidity.

The miniatures of the Berlin album show that as early as the beginning of the fourteenth century we can speak of a naturalistic style as well as an abstract one. In the sequel naturalistic trends prevail, and the narrative style of representation found in the early *Shahname* illustrations begins gradually to be superseded by a descriptive style. The famous Demotte *Shahname* (1340)[111] with its fifty-eight miniatures in large format reflects this development as a work of the transitional period. The epic manner of representation here reaches its peak, even though the rendering of the figures, their dress and the scenery offers much scope for descriptive painting. The *Shahname* illustrations of the Topkapu Museum dating from 1370 have, on the other hand, an *50* explicitly descriptive character; the narrative here allows of a very full representation of the surrounding landscape, which draws the figures into its domain in an unusual fashion. With the Timurid period a new phase in the stylistic development of the *Shahname* illustrations begins; this we will call the decorative style. Though the principles for the composition are still the old ones, the original types of figures are now transformed into motifs for decorative ornament.[112] The creative powers begin to atrophy in this play of forms and colours: the succeeding period brings nothing new, so that we can scarcely any longer speak of an organic development of style in the *Shahname* illustrations of the fifteenth and sixteenth centuries.

PICTURES OF WAR

Illustrations to Rashid-ed-Din's World Chronicle

About 1300 Rashid-ed-Din, vizier of the Mongol rulers Gazan and Oljaitu, wrote his *World Chronicle (Jami-et-Tawarikh)* on the grand scale and had it illustrated with an abundance of pictures. The principle subjects were Biblical legends and episodes from Islamic and Chinese history, among which those from the lives of Buddha and Mohammed deserve special attention. The illustrated parts of the work are to be found nowadays in Edinburgh (UBN 20, dated 1307), in London (Royal Asiatic Society, No. 59 Fol., dated 1314) and in Istanbul (Topkapu Sarayi Muzesi, dated 1314). The Istanbul edition is in the historical work *Majma-et-Tawarikh* (Hazine 1653, 1654) compiled by Hajiz-i-Abru in 1425. To these meanwhile were added forty-six further miniatures from the Berlin volumes of bound collections (Diez A. Fol. 70–72); these show a close affinity in style with the pictures in the part that we know of Rashid-ed-Din's universal history, and in all probability are illustrations to a missing part of this work in which, to judge by the themes treated, the history of the Mongols should have been set forth.[113]

The style of the *Jami-et-Tawarikh* illustrations is called Chinese-Mongol in the traditional terminology of the art-historian. This designation signifies that we are concerned with works which, in contrast to the Seljuk-Mongol, are much indebted to Far Eastern art, and in which the contribution of the Near East is hardly traceable any more. The characteristic of this style is that it gives great prominence to line in obtaining its effects. The pictures of this group are drawn directly with fine brushstrokes on the paper, then lightly coloured in such a way as to avoid over-painting in other colours. They often give the impression of monochrome drawing. But they are not always that. Among these illustrations there are pages which show rather more delight in colour and in which the scale of colour appears strongly differentiated and richer in contrast. But for all that a different significance attaches to colour from that found in Seljuk-Mongol miniature painting. There, forms and colours can never be separated from one another: the colour is swallowed up by the miniatures and as it were absorbed. In our pages, on the other hand, it appears in the form of localised spots and is simply used as a means to an end—namely, to enhance the power of the drawing. Here it is made to rank neither equal with, nor indeed above line, but is subordinated to it. The pictures of these pages are nearer in style and execution to drawing than to miniatures, and therefore it would not be wrong to treat them as coloured drawings.[114]

The new realism of the Mongols, deeply indebted as it was to the naturalistic tradition of Far Eastern painting, could assert itself better in the illustrations to the *World Chronicle*, which within its framework as a work of history was intended more to retain the character of an illustrated document than it could in the *Shahname*. It was a novelty for that time that line, which in the Islamic as well as in the Christian art of the Middle Ages was a means of abstraction intended to reduce the body to a flat surface, now produced an effect of plastic modelling by means of a sensitively controlled variation in thickness. Shading also contributes much to this modelling effect, since it makes the surfaces change over short distances from hard to soft and from dark to light, particularly in the folds of clothing so full of curves. Thanks to this play of

8 The Capture of a Town

9 Stampeded Horses

10 Cavalry Pursuit

50

shadows, which is always adapted to the lines of the drawing, the artist could arouse in the beholder a strong sense of volume, unknown in the Near East before the Mongol period. Among the illustrations to the *World Chronicle* those in the bound collections of Berlin are the least known. There the range of subjects comprises mainly scenes of war, but also court ceremonies, at which the ruler, or the ruler with his wife, appears amid his courtiers, and lastly a few scenes from the legends of the prophets. In their formal arrangement the court ceremonies adopt a plan of composition which later became prevalent and was then generally used in similar court-scenes. In the much later *Jami-et-Tawarikh* manuscripts of the Bibliothèque Nationale (Suppl. Pers. 1113) and of the Asiatic Society of Bengal (No. D.31), in which, as in the *Tarikh-i-Gazan Khan* of Rashid-ed-Din, the history of the Mongols is treated, we see a series of such scenes. The battle-pieces provide the liveliest scenes of our group. Warriors squeezed into iron mail, riders with their heads drawn back between their shoulders and mounted on 'flying horses', form densely packed groups which, ranged diagonally and often distributed in the manner of scatter-patterns over the surface, threaten to burst open the frame of the picture. These pages convey the impression of an elemental power that, once unleashed amid all this tumult, cannot be held down. The composition in these representations develops in a definite direction. The best examples are provided by the scenes of pursuit. If the result is an antithetical arrangement of the picture, this is only in order to strengthen the effect of movement by the contrast of its directions, an *10* effect uniquely illustrated here. *9*

In contrast to the *Shahname* illustrations, the war-scenes of the *World Chronicle* have the character of crowd-scenes, in which individual items scarcely count. The prince or the commander is the sole exception. The rest are members of a whole, they appear in groups and act in groups like one man acting under orders. These *8* pictures are not concerned to show a course of events in which persons can act by their own will. The figures here are rather like marionettes whose movements are restricted to a few motifs only, such as flight, attack, pursuit, or the bearing of archers in battle, but being carried out in groups, they exercise an extraordinary power of suggestion on the beholder.

THE FIGURE OF THE RULER AS SYMBOL OF POWER

In one of the famous Saray albums in Istanbul is a picture of a Mongol ruler which deserves special attention because of its iconographical content as well as its artistic quality. The picture covers a double spread of two full pages. On the right the prince is shown in ceremonial style, surrounded by an array of courtiers *11* He sits, a goblet of intoxicating drink in his hand, on a golden throne of state adorned with Far Eastern designs of leaves and flowers, its back ornamented with two free-standing dragons' heads with closed jaws. The figure of the prince, which dominates the whole picture in strict frontality, towers above those about him. Yet two figures are marked off from the rest by their size; they occupy places on either side of the throne. According to the description of a Mongol *kurultay* (ceremonial audience) given by Marco Polo in his *Travels* the female figure may be identified as his mother or his wife, while the other figure on the right of the throne may be the crown prince or a high dignitary. The emphasis on the central row of figures leads to a division of the whole surface of the picture into three. In the upper part two winged genii hold scarves, and between the dense throngs of courtiers two men hold a sword and a bunch of flowers over the ruler's head, which is adorned with a nimbus. In the lower part a banqueting scene is shown, at which musicians, playing various instruments, and dancers provide entertainment.

51

11   A Ruler Enthroned

12   Gayumart, the First King, in the Mountains

p. 99 On the opposite, or left-hand page, a triumphal procession is shown in which two opposing files of riders with hunting hawks, half-naked youths, various animals, and fabulous creatures including a winged unicorn, take part as an act of homage. The triumphal procession is moving in the king's direction, thus establishing a meaningful connection between the two pages.

To judge by other such representations, these pictures are in fact the frontispieces of a manuscript;[115] since this is missing, however, and the pictures have no inscription, we do not know who is represented here. But even if we knew it the identification could not be taken literally. For in such pictures very little trouble was taken to make the portrait like the person represented. With regard to the Turkish overlords of the Near East, a Mongolian ruler type with slit eyes and round face was developed in painting, one which the artists imposed like a mask on every prince they painted. So too the painter of our picture of a ruler sees in his prince not as the man of flesh and blood, but as the bearer of royal power, to be shown in his full glory only as a symbolical figure. Thus what we behold is a symbol of authority, indicated by the most various signs of supreme rank, such as the triumphal procession, the seated position on the throne, the aureole, the figures of angels crowning the ruler, the weapons and even the banqueting scene and the goblet in the royal hand. The goblet expresses in visible form the unbridled indulgence of the court circle; for the Oriental, enjoyment of life and the love of display were among the royal privileges inseparable from the idea of power.

Although our pages belong to the tradition of rulers' portraits of the Near East, they constitute a showpiece of Mongol painting about 1300; they enable us to appreciate what the art of the Near East owed to its Mongol conquerors. The late antique tradition of the Central Asian frescoes of Turkestan is to be seen here in all its grandeur. Within the rigid compositional scheme determined by the heraldic symmetry of old Sassanid art there is everywhere a breath of new life. Only the frilled folds of the ruler's richly adorned apparel betray an element of style that recalls the old Baghdad School. The rendering of men and animals, on the other hand, is evidence of a genuine feeling for nature which was unknown to the pre-Mongol period. Central Asian too is the division of the picture's surface into bands, adorned with scattered flowers, and also the nearly monochrome colouring dominated by red and yellow; close investigation would show that even the iconographical motifs for the most part originate from the frescoes of the former Uighur empire, as one can see from the very various forms of headdress and from the king's helmet, which looks like a bluebell and occurs in this form in the Central Asian paintings of Turfan from the seventh century.

The Mongols, with their realistic approach, had no appreciation of many of these marks of rank or attributes of power which were inseparable from the Near Eastern picture of a ruler, so that about the middle of the fourteenth century these lost their significance or simply disappeared. A new ruler-image was created, of which we have a fine example in another album of the Saray Library. This figure comes from a lost *Book* 12 *of Kings* and represents Gayumart, the first king, in the mountains. The ceremonial picture is transformed into a narrative scene in which the deeds of heroes are recorded. The artist does indeed still hold fast to the original symmetrical scheme of composition of the Near Eastern pictures of rulers, but the whole scene is removed from the abstract background sparkling with gold and set in a naturalistically rendered landscape, where a niche-like hollow in the body of a massive tree-stump serves the king as a throne. The ceremonial picture in this case recalls the rendering of a royal hunt. The faces, postures and gestures of the various figures are none of them alike, and the group, in its unusual dress verging on the grotesque, gives the effect of a parody of the former Near Eastern picture of a ruler. The only elements of iconography which can be explained as symbols of authority (or rather), force, are, apart from the panther-skin sur-coats of the ruler and his attendants, the frightening beasts at their feet, which appeared also in many pre-Mongol pictures of rulers, though there admittedly in heraldic arrangement.

ILLUSTRATIONS TO WORKS OF LIGHT LITERATURE

Until the Mongol period the governing classes in China and Persia were also the representatives of higher culture. After the founding of the empire it was different: in the occupied countries the classes which had hitherto ruled lost their importance, and the general result was, more obviously in Persia than in China, that cultural life was reduced to a popular level. One of the consequences of this transformation is that the vernacular begins to take the place of the difficult literary language, and a literature of entertainment develops, which in comparison with writing of higher quality gains continually in importance. Among the works of this type of literature were the adventure stories and seafarers' yarns which were abundantly illustrated. We reproduce here two pictures from among these illustrations, one showing a man among

13   Visit to the Hermit

14   The Seven Sleepers

15, 16   monkeys, the other a brawl in a boat. These miniatures relate to two stories; further episodes of the same stories are to be found in Istanbul and Tübingen.[116] They all show the preference of that age for scenes of crude rowdiness and peculiar adventures which at times border on the obscene (Diez A. Fol. 71, p. 12).

    Arabic literature offered the illustrators an abundant supply of fantastic themes for their creations. One may quote here Qasvini's *The Miracles of Creation* or Sindbad's Voyages in the *Thousand and One Nights*. It is to be assumed that the illustrators of light literature took their subjects largely from such works. Representations of *Hariri* executed in the Mongol style are not known to us. On the other hand the *Kalila and Dimna*

17, 18   illustrations in the University Library at Istanbul from the year 1370 show that the animal stories outlived the Mongol period. The subject of love was extremely popular; the earliest known representations of Khusrau and Shirin come from this period (Diez A. Fol. 71, p. 6). Among religious themes the Mongols

14   took the greatest delight in the legend of the 'Seven Sleepers'. The life of potentates, their pleasures at court, garden-scenes, hunting and games, audiences and princely visits must, to judge by the surviving illustrations, have been the focus of interest for all.

13   From this milieu comes an illustration representing one of the earliest versions of the 'Visit to the Hermit' (middle of the fourteenth century), which was later to become the stock theme of miniature painting.

56

15   The Man among the Monkeys

There was an inexhaustible source of such themes in the oriental versions of the *Alexander Romance*, which, as is well known, was put into verse in the *Iskandarname*, one of the five *Khamsa* or epic-romantic works of Nizami. We have, further, in the Saray albums of the Berlin and Istanbul collections an abundance of *Shahname* illustrations that show a rather provincial and popular style. The *Shahname* manuscripts which were once accompanied by these illustrations certainly had the character of popular editions. Their inferior quality and great number indicate serial productions which were very probably turned out in workshops formed for the purpose.[117]

The conversion to naturalism to be observed everywhere in Near Eastern art in the fourteenth century is very noticeable in all these illustrations. This naturalism seems very nearly to supersede the decorative two-dimensional style of Islamic miniature-painting. The surrounding landscape is no longer mere scene-painting but is genuine space, possessing distance and depth, in which the figures stand and move with absolute freedom. The quality of such representations was as a whole undistinguished. But through these illustrations the Mongol style became universally known and could gain currency in the remotest provinces.

16 Fight in a Boat

17 Battle of the Crows and the Owls

18   The Donkey and the Jackal

RELIGIOUS PAINTING AND EARLY REPRESENTATIONS OF HEAVEN
The Master Ahmed Musa

In the central Asian homeland of the Mongols, as is clear from the frescoes of East Turkestan, painting was deeply rooted in religion and thereby had a sacred significance. When the Mongols reached the west they found a form of painting which was divided from religion by an unbridgeable gulf. The reason for this divorce was the religion of Islam. The personification of God in pictures was so far contrary to its abstract conception of Him, that artists in Islamic lands did not venture on religious themes at all. When the Mongols embraced Islam, this was changed. The religious ban was henceforward applied only to the representation of God. Religious themes on the other hand were taken into the artists' repertory without regard for the pious horror which Sunnite circles felt for their embodiment in pictures. Thus a religious form of painting arose even in the Islamic lands of the west.

At first religious themes were illustrated within the framework of historical writings. Thus, for example Rashid-ed-Din's *World Chronicle* contains a rich collection of religious pictures. But gradually interest in such pictures grew so much that religious texts, intended to edify Mohammedans, were illustrated. Among the most important texts of this kind were the *Prophets' Biographies (Qisas el enbiya)* and the story of *Moham-*

60

med's Ascension (Mi'rajname). From the fifteenth and sixteenth centuries we have a rich collection of such illustrated manuscripts, but from the Mongol period very few have been preserved. Among these rare works we should mention in the first place the Ascension scenes in one of the Saray albums (Hazine 2154) in the Topkapu Museum. They comprise a series of miniatures in large format ascribed to the master *19–24* Ahmed Musa. Ettinghausen dates these pages to the second quarter of the fourteenth century, and if this is correct, they represent the oldest version of the known representations of the Ascension.

Apart from these pictures, this bound collection contains other works and a notable commentary by Dust Mohammed, a well-known chronicler of the sixteenth century. He gives a legendary account of the early history of painting in Persia, and follows this with a convincing survey of the schools of painting under the last khans as far as the Jala'irs. In this connection we are told who Ahmed Musa was; according to Dust Mohammed, it was he who in the time of Abu Sa'id (1317–35) 'lifted the veil from the face of painting and invented the new style of painting'. Among the works of the master[118] Dust Mohammed mentions a *Mi'rajname* copied by Mawlana Abdullah. Are our representations of the Ascension and these illustrations to the *Mi'rajname* mentioned by Dust Mohammed one and the same? Are the miniatures of the Saray album authentic works of the master Ahmed Musa who is extolled in Persia as the inventor of the new style of painting? This is not ruled out by the date of origin for the pages that Ettinghausen gives. But unfortunately we have nothing to prove it.

Illustrated manuscripts usually contain a reference to the masters from whose hand the pictures came. But the hand-writing which belonged with our miniature no longer exists. Some of the manuscripts that are preserved have an inscription according to which they are 'works of the master Ahmed Musa', but such ascriptions to renowned masters are commonplace in the east, and the authenticity of these inscriptions may justly be doubted. That Dust Mohammed's commentary and the Ascensions of which he speaks occur in one and the same volume might perhaps be regarded as authenticating the ascription. But in the production of the bound collections, which were called *muraqqa* (patchwork or pastework), no objective principle of arrangement was followed and it may easily be that this combination is an accident.

The lost text to which our miniatures once belonged may have diverged in many points from the Ascension manuscripts that we know. In our pictures, for example, we see the Prophet borne by the archangel Gabriel *21, 22* over waters and mountains, although according to the usual tradition he embarked on his journey under the archangel's guidance on the back of the fabulous beast Burak. *24*

The scene with the heavenly cock is again quite unusual. The giant form of a cock is shown, enthroned *20* on a high base, shining white against a background of darkened silver. Before the throne the angels in compact rows are praying devoutly. There is no doubt that the cock in this picture has a divine significance. In Iran, the cock, as watcher of the first rays of dawn, was considered sacred. Ostensibly we have here a motif that is Mazdaistic in origin and later passed into the stock of images used by Islamic art. In the architectural sculpture of the Near East we often meet the cock in ornamentation. But in our picture it is not an ornamental motif; it is the chief figure represented in what might be described as a scene of worship. But the worship of animals is contrary to Islam, and our miniature is concerned with an episode mentioned in the tradition of the Ascension, in which a cock of giant size as herald of the light proclaims the Muslim hour of prayer.

The other representations show the Prophet in the Dome of the Rock in Jerusalem, that is, in the place where according to tradition his Ascension began; also two scenes of his reception in Heaven, two scenes

19   The Prophet with the Archangel Gabriel in Heaven

20   The Heavenly Cock

23   of Paradise and finally the scene in which an angel is handing to him the model of a town.[119] The last picture refers to an apocalyptic vision of the Prophet, in which, as a traditional text or *hadish* tells us, he foretells the coming conquest of Constantinople by a great Muslim ruler.

In these representations we have certainly no more than a part of the stock of pictures that once existed. But the material at our disposal does enable us to see that we are dealing with an artist who was well versed in the epic tradition of oriental painting. He is a storyteller and is primarily concerned with recording in pictures a fable handed down by tradition. This is expressly indicated by those pictures in which the Prophet, accompanied by Gabriel, appears simply as a marginal figure: as a beholder and narrator, through whose mediation we are permitted to share in the marvellous events which befall him on his Ascension. Thus the artist reproduces what tradition recounts from the mouth of the Prophet, and because in the Islamic view the Prophet is only a man—not the son of God but his slave—his visions are seen in the picture through human eyes and represented in perfectly credible fashion. The scenes indeed take place in the heavenly sphere but are subject to earthly laws. Heavenly events, like earthly ones, are rendered in temporal and spatial terms.

62

21   Mohammed above the Mountains

The only sign of sacredness that appears in these pictures is the aureole round the head of the Prophet, which in the shape of a flaming *mandorla* surrounds the entire figure of Mohammed in the scene where the town is handed to him. In the representation of the angels the wings and the serrated Sassanid crown alone indicate that we are in the presence of the transcendental. The solid physique of the divine messenger gives him an earth-bound quality, and the long plaits, like the Mongol dress with its short-sleeved over-garment, are exactly in the fashion of the time. The picture's composition, the grouping of the figures in space, the rendering of architecture, landscape, movement and attitude recall the works of the early Italian Renaissance, and certainly these pictures are not entirely free from western influence. Scholarship today thinks it possible that Dante's work was influenced by Islamic legends of heavenly journeys, and conversely, that a strong impulse from the works of the Italian masters can be traced in the Ascension scenes ascribed to the celebrated Ahmed Musa. Such mutual influences cannot be explained by purely external relations between east and west: they rather presuppose a common field of resonance. It seems that at the end of the Middle Ages the east too, though by a route quite different from the west, reached the threshold of a Renaissance, which however was checked by the power of the iconoclastic attitude in Islam and brought to a halt from the very outset.

22   The Prophet above the Water

23　Presentation of a Town

24   The Ascension of Mohammed

In the Saray albums of the Topkapu Museum are included not only representations of the Ascension but a series of pictures which are preserved for us as loose leaves torn out of various religious manuscripts. These deserve to be studied individually. Here we wish to refer to two examples only from this bundle of sheets, which represent two different phases in the development of the Mongol style in the fourteenth

25 century. In the one example Abraham's sacrifice is shown. The scenery of the landscape has more importance here than in representations of the Ascension. The method is not merely narrative but also descriptive. The manner of rendering rocks and plants is closely akin to that of the *Kalila and Dimna* illustrations in the University Library at Istanbul, and the page, like those illustrations, was probably produced in the second half

26 of the fourteenth century, say about 1370. The other sheet shows a young prince being carried off by an angel. Here the simple method of pictorial narrative is still very much alive, but the landscape is no longer free from decorative additions, a fact which foreshadows the coming Timurid style. This page was probably made a few decades later than the preceding one, say toward the end of the fourteenth century.

66

25   Abraham's Sacrifice

26   An Angel Carries off a
Young Prince

67

27   The Angels' Battle with the Dragons

PICTURES OF DEMONS AND SCENES FROM THE LIFE OF THE NOMADS

In recent years a group of drawings was found in one of the Saray albums of the Topkapu Museum which in their style and iconographical content differ unmistakably from the illuminations that we know in the Mongol style and form a group by themselves. In spite of the effects of time, which make some drawings almost unrecognizable, they point to one of the greatest masters of Mongol painting. About the artist himself we know nothing. No historical source mentions him. We do not even know his correct name, for the name Ustad Mehmed Siyah Qalem (Master Mehmed, named the Black Pen) which occurs here and there on his pictures, does not look as though it were the signature of his own hand. Time seems to have dealt unsparingly with this artist. The only traces of his having lived are his drawings.[120]

The Mongol miniatures we have so far treated are illustrations to various manuscripts which were written in Arabic and Persian. The paintings of Siyah Qalem cannot be fitted into this series. The subjects represented come from a world which has found no annalist among the literary sources. In these pictures we come to know the life of the steppe, the life of people who have nothing settled, comfortable, or townlike about them. They go barefoot, dance like savages, gesture crudely, and live a simple life in the company of their beasts. And all this is set out in Siyah Qalem's drawings, with a realism bordering on brutality, in a manner so authentic

28   Illustration to an East Asian Folktale

and close to life that we may assume that these pictures come from the hand of a master native to the world of the steppes. A literary counterpart to this realism is found in the *Secret History*, which is unique in Mongol Letters. That is not to say that Siyah Qalem's drawings are illustrations to such a work; for although they show a unity of style, they vary greatly among themselves: they are painted in one or more colours on parchment or silk; some pictures are cut out of larger rolls; and the scale of the pictures varies between 12.5 × 13 cm. and 22.5 × 48 cm. This is evidence that these pictures cannot be illustrations to a book. But to judge from the method of representation, the master who created these sheets cannot have lacked literary models: we may guess that they were old epic texts for recitation, widely current in popular poetry.

The pictures of Siyah Qalem may be divided according to their iconographical content into two groups: religious pictures and representations of nomad life.

The subjects of the first group come from a world of ideas which is strange to the monotheistic religions; they are closely connected with shamanism. The chief figures are demons which can be defined as peculiar hybrid monsters. They are distinguished from human beings by their horns, tails, hides, terrifying travesties of faces and other animal and demon attributes which rest like masks on their solidly built human

29–34

29   Donkey with Two Demons   30   Two Demon Musicians

bodies. At any rate these monsters are very like human beings and behave in a similar manner; they fight and dance, play musical instruments, carry off people and horses, lead an emaciated beast on the rein and sacrifice a horse as an act of worship to an unknown god. Even their clothing is like human clothing: they wear aprons and have gold rings at their necks, hand and feet. Their bodies are tense even in attitudes of rest, and the overflowing energy in their limbs is always ready to expend itself. They arouse in us the impression of a malevolent and irrational power such as discharges itself in the roll of thunder or in the bellowing of wild beasts. A few demon figures directly recall the fantastic creations of Gothic, and we must not forget that these monstrous creatures were both for Christians and for Mohammedans definitely on the side of the powers of evil, of the devil or of the damned. If they are interpreted as creations of a religious imagination, they are still not to be grasped through any antithetical conception of good and evil, Paradise and Hell, heaven and earth. We must imagine, rather, some pagan religion which makes demonic powers of the secret forces of nature and at the same time tries to exorcise them. Perhaps these pictures should be taken as personifications of such powers and it is possible that some of them represent masked shamans who imitate demons and do battle with them for the deliverance of men and beasts.

31 Demon Carrying off a Horse

32   Horse Sacrifice

33   Dancing Demons

34   The Fight with the Demon

35–47   The second group portrays the hard life of the nomads. The feet of people who are perpetually on the move are shown in these pictures as vividly as their faces. They move barefoot from place to place and with their beasts lead a life full of privations. In their rough world there is no place for the charming and the idyllic. It is only rarely that we find drawings where the artist depicts a nomad camp at rest or a peaceful scene of
43, 41 family life. But even then Siyah Qalem's realism loses nothing of its harshness. Everything is shown in the same rough nakedness that we know from his other pictures. We get the impression from this group that they portray the very people whose imaginative world was the subject of the demon pictures.

It is distinctive of Siyah Qalem's method that in his drawings the figures are cut loose from their natural surroundings and appear as if on a smooth white painting surface without any depth. They are always placed at a certain distance from one another and are brought into mutual contact by means of conventional signs – a look, a movement of the hand or head. There is a likeness, not to be ignored, between the drawings and the
35, 37 scenes of a shadow-play. Here too the appearance of the characters seems to be more important than their actions. This goes so far that isolated groups stand out like motionless scenes from a drama whose action is unknown to us. We get a distinct impression that these might be connected with the theatre, particularly on account of the many conversation scenes. This is enhanced by the figures that recall masked actors. Their

74

35 Giant Sup-
porting himself
on a Staff

faces express astonishment mixed with fear or anger. The hard and fixed looks, always the same, which we find in the most diverse scenes, never express a personal state of mind. We are presented with grimacing masks and not with real faces at all. Again, the movement of the body, the arms, the hands and even the feet is rendered in a stylized manner. Gait and gestures vary but little from one figure to another. In all situations we have characters, precisely defined by facial expression, miming, gestures and costume, who are in a state of high dramatic tension. Even the most peaceful scenes are charged with latent passions; in every one something portentous is happening.

40, 42

It would be appropriate to describe Siyah Qalem as a painter of representative or hieratic subjects. The richness of natural forms and the joy of description seem to have been unknown to him. If he shows a nomad camp, he gives us a number of visual forms scattered almost at random over the surface, which do not catch men, beasts and objects in their everyday appearance but transmit a series of separately stylized images from memory. Renderings of landscape are lacking among Siyah Qalem's drawings. If a piece of nature does for once appear, which is very rare, it is again a symbol that indicates a stage property. Thus Siyah Qalem's idiom of drawing is nearly always confined to the typical. The figures which he paints represent general types and never give us a picture of an individual. He uses a few basic patterns for his faces, whose expression varies little from one person to another. Nature in Siyah Qalem, however near to reality, remains always abstract and deliberate. A few drawings of animals might suggest direct contact with nature, but there too

43

34

36   Quarry

37   Conversation Scene

the painter is held back by a received tradition from surrendering himself altogether to any sort of personal observation. Behind the surprising realism of the horse we soon detect an abstract synthetic conception. As *45* everywhere else, the feet here are seen systematically from two opposite sides and the head, which is taken from several angles, appears just as abstract as a drawing by Picasso.

In spite of this abstraction, Siyah Qalem still takes the nature of things into account. For him abstraction is not a flight from nature as it is, say, among the artists of Islam. Although his creations are presented outside the context of the surrounding world, they are still conceived in all their reality. In contrast to the weightless figures of the miniatures, the body here has a sculptural monumentality which expresses genuine and convincing weight. This weight explains the impression of size which these figures create even in the pictures *38* drawn on the smallest scale. If the figures seem to float free in the air and their feet never to come into contact with the ground, there are still very few painters whose human beings stand so firm on their feet and appear so heavy as his. In this connection the pose of resting the weight on a traveller's staff, a motif which

Siyah Qalem often repeats, is specially characteristic. No matter whether they are lifting a load, fighting one another, sitting down or simply standing, the figures attach so firmly to the ground that their whole strength seems to be derived from their weight. Their feet are club-like members into which Siyah Qalem compresses the entire energy of his giants. Everything presses down against the ground and everything shoots up from it. Even the dance does not free the body from the ground but shows how the ground draws the body to

33, 39   it, so that the weight of the former is again made very obvious. Whether they sit or crouch, the figures all have one inclination: to spread themselves upon the ground and to occupy the greatest possible area on it.

38   The legs open as though they wished to clasp the ground which is invisible but always so strongly present.

The weight of which we speak appears in Siyah Qalem as the visible manifestation of a power dwelling in men and must not be confused with inert matter. For that reason Siyah Qalem can keep the bodies of his

38 The Crouching Giant

39   Dancing Shamans

colossi remarkably light in spite of their massiveness. Though the bodies press with their full weight on the ground they are, even when at rest, always in a state of tension and movement, always ready to leap up springily and to stretch and strain their limbs. Altogether, Siyah Qalem's drawing is always particularly intensive when concerned with the movable parts of the body and the centres of physical strength. The limbs are specially emphasised in his drawings: elbows and knees have exaggerated swellings; the muscles are charged with energy, and the feet always tense like the pads and claws of wild creatures. Thanks to these expressive emphases the slightest movement has an astonishing breadth and realism. When a man is resting upon a staff, we feel the whole weight of his body; the mere gripping or carrying of an object brings into play the great physical strength which it is Siyah Qalem's greatest concern to express. Often we are actually put in mind of Michelangelo's giants, in spite of all the other ways in which the two artists differ from one another. Have not both the same passionate interest in the dynamism of the human body? Certainly the strength of Michelangelo's giants, held in check by a rational geometrical ordering, acquires a peaceful, harmonious majesty; while in Siyah Qalem we are confronted with a force, tumultuously released, which cares nothing for grace and measure. However that may be, there is common to both a striving to catch the movement and dynamism of the body, a striving which brings a loosening and dissolution of its mass.

40 Standing Men in Conversation

41 Nomad Family

42 Nomads

39, 46 Arms, hands and feet often enter a twisting motion in which the fixed form of the body is transformed into a pattern in space. Thus Siyah Qalem's figures, though they are torn from their natural setting, create their own space; they are actually in that space.

The means that Siyah Qalem uses to achieve a three-dimensional effect is line. True, contrasted shading also helps to soften and round the shapes in his drawings. Yet what at first appears as modelling can be reduced ultimately to a virtuosity in the use of line which cares nothing for the requirements of perspective. Line remains Siyah Qalem's most characteristic means of expression; it alone enables him to render his anatomical observations. He uses it to convey folds, wrinkles, relief and raised surfaces of all kinds. The play of shadows, which is nearly always arbitrary, is used as a further means of reinforcing the effect of line, but can never replace it in expressing volume. The same procedure is often employed in a *pointilliste* manner to render the texture of skin or clothing. The fact that Siyah Qalem is not absolutely obliged to use this procedure to round his shapes and make them pass into one another, but can do without it, shows that no new technique is involved as, say, in the *sfumato* of Leonardo da Vinci.

It is no accident that the folds in clothing remind one of Gothic, which likewise uses linear means to *40, 42* create plastic values. The inheritance from late antiquity is just as noticeable in Siyah Qalem's paintings as in Gothic statues. Here too the drawing is often no more than a stream of parallel rhythmical lines which blurs all details of the costume. But this very comparison shows how different the two worlds were, each

82

43   Nomad Camp

44   A Nomad Leads his Emaciated Horse by the Bridle

83

dominated and shaped by a different spirit. While the Christian spirit aims at withdrawing substance from the bodies by the play of folds, the heathen spirit of the Mongol artist uses the flowing waves of the clothing as moulds into which he forces his figures, to take on life. In Gothic the lines spread out from a knot and thence proceed to dissolve the body; here in contrast they cover it over with spirals: heavy sacks are formed pressing downward towards the ground, by which means the solid form of the body acquires its three-dimensional appearance. In contrast to the Gothic figures, which follow the soaring lines of the cathedral, the figures in Siyah Qalem grow broader and more massive downwards.

The date and place of origin of the Siyah Qalem pages are still debated. They are certainly not Persian. For they appear to have been uninfluenced by the Persian-Mongol tradition in art. The style, as already indicated, is representative rather than descriptive, and appears to be entirely unaffected by all the naturalistic achievements of the fourteenth century, which we find generally in the works of Mongol art in the Near East. Moreover, the iconography of these pictures, which present the heathen past of the Mongols so genuinely and convincingly, suggests that their place of origin lay beyond the immediate range of Islamic

45   A Nomad Grazes his Horse

influence, and we should perhaps look for it nearer to the Mongol homeland. The Siyah Qalem pages must in any case have originated in a region which was open to Chinese influence and where the nomad peoples of the steppes had not yet lost their distinctive character. Turkestan and Transoxania are such regions. At the same time, the Siyah Qalem pages are marked off by certain 'archaisms' from all known works of the Chinese-Mongol tradition, so that in them we can find no solid ground for their dating. For a long time conjectures varied between 'earlier than 1200' and the second half of the sixteenth century. Ettinghausen dates these pages to the fifteenth century,[121] and that in particular on account of a blueish-white porcelain vessel in a drawing by Siyah Qalem (Freer Gallery of Art, No. 37, 25) of a type which is said to occur not earlier than this time. This dating is supported by a picture showing a conjuration-scene in the Topkapu Museum (Hazine 2153, p. 37a) painted in the same *pointilliste* style as the one just mentioned, which in the manner of its rendering of a lump of rock and of a few plant and flower motifs already presents stylistic features that mark the Timurid period. Hence we may conclude that this page too originated about 1400. With this established, we are in a far better position to date the other Siyah Qalem pages, from which our book gives only a se-

46   A Horse is Groomed

47 Warrior with Horse

lection. These pictures are very closely linked in style with the two dated pages, and we may assume that they are all the work of the same master. The page depicting demon musicians (Ill. 30) is in fact only a variant of that in the Freer Gallery, and the two pictures agree in their *mise-en-scène* as also in the motifs of the postures and movements of the demons. True, the group of nomad pictures differs in its range of colour and technical execution from the representations of demons, but the differences lose their importance beside the peculiarities of style they have in common; and even if we had to concede that they were by different hands, the works would not be far separated in date. In short, we should allow a period of fifty or sixty years for the Siyah Qalem pages, divided between the fourteenth and fifteenth centuries.

We know nothing of the pictorial tradition on which the art of Mehmed Siyah Qalem rested. For this reason we are not yet able to decide where the master's personal contribution begins and when the pictorial tradition to which he is bound came to an end. So far as we know his works, they reveal an independent spirit and an adaptation which was imposed upon it. Probably we are dealing with an artist who lived among a nomad people and, in company with them, responded to new influences; an artist of the Central Asian Turco-Mongol tribes of nomads, who originally brought not only the forms of art but also the manners and customs of Far Eastern cultures to Western Asia, and yet adapted them to new circumstances, and remodelled them or enriched them with new experiences.

From the few drawings which are included in the Saray albums we come to know the nomads and their art from a surprising new angle. In these pictures the pre-Islamic heathen world of ideas belonging to Sha-manism takes on an exuberance that we meet nowhere else. This exuberance is carried so far in ritual acts, that the characters shown in one of the drawings dismember a horse in the course of their dance and wave *32* its limbs, still dripping with blood, round themselves like scarves. No heavenly spirit visits this world, where brutal and elemental power is at large in the form of unleashed monsters. A few figures of angels alone appear round the edges of the illustrations to East Asian folk-tales; the representation of a battle on *28* the grand scale, in which angels bind the dragons in the abyss, belongs by its iconographical content clearly *27* to the world of Buddhist belief. Though this art is indebted to the Far East, we find in it no trace of the impressionistic lyricism of East Asian painting. Its linear and *pointilliste* refinement, which the master Siyah Qalem owes to the Chinese masters, he puts at the service of a brutal realism which cares little for a pleasant effect. There is a barbaric quality about the Siyah Qalem pages which cannot be harmonised with the aesthetic of East Asia. Such realism was alien to the very nature of Islam and could only cause uneasiness in the Islamic world. This might explain why the work of the master had no successors in Islamic lands and is a unique phenomenon.

LANDSCAPE PAINTING, DRAWINGS OF ANIMALS

In Persia the feeling for nature had deep roots reaching back to Zoroastrian concepts and became wide-spread later through the pantheistic doctrine of Sufism. But the resources of this country were insufficient for it to achieve any pictorial representation of nature, and it was only when the seeds of East Asian art fell on Persia's fertile ground that a new style of landscape painting, hitherto unknown in the Near East, could arise.

From the initial period of this art form not much is preserved, but we may count a few works from the Saray albums as belonging to it. They appear to have been painted about the middle of the fourteenth century. Among them we should mention the *Autumn Landscape* in Tübingen, in which the melancholy of dying nature is conveyed in masterly fashion by a few withered trees, a river and bare brushwood (Diez A. Fol. 71, p. 10).[122] Human and animal figures do not appear in this picture, so that we are justified in calling it a pure landscape, in which nature is no longer merely accessory but forms the object of artistic creation in its own right. Though the *Summer Picture* in Istanbul is preserved only as a fragment, it must, to judge by its brilliant *pointilliste* execution, be the work of an important artist. Like the Tübingen page, it offers a bird's-eye view of nature; this creates a sort of panorama that conceals within itself both distances and depths. The scope of the picture in these landscapes becomes smaller as soon as the artist's interest moves from the fulness of nature to concentrate on a few forms. The artists who painted these landscapes knew that the sense of depth in space in a picture could be expressed most tellingly by bringing out the contrast between a close and a distant view. That this was so is evident from some of the pictures of the albums, where there is often a close-up view of a single bird occupying the foreground. Play with perspective was obviously widespread at this time: the artists sought to treat nature from continually fresh points of view, enabling them to win from her new and surprising aspects which enriched landscape painting beyond anything previously imagined. Mountain landscapes enjoyed a general popularity at this time; a well-preserved example is now in Tübingen (Diez A. Fol. 71, p. 28).[123] The picture shows a landscape surrounded by high, steep walls of rock, in which the grandeur and loneliness of nature is brought home with particular effect by the single figure of a rider in the foreground. In the landscapes of this period the screens of rock are a principal motif, filling out, dividing up, building up and walling off; blocks piled one upon another result in fantastic formations. From a distance the effect of this configuration is one of uniformity and the surface of the rocks shows a smooth structure, as if cleft by an axe. But if these rock-formations are shown close at

48   Bird in a Rocky Landscape

49   Summer Landscape

50 Iskandar's Fight with the Wolves

hand, the whole is broken up into countless single elements which assume peculiar, bizarre forms. A crude sketching replaces the modelling here. Dark lines edged with white separate and join together the masses *13* of stone, and the rendering of the rough, spongy, porous texture of tufa seems to have given particular pleasure to the Mongol sense of reality.

Gnarled tree-trunks and jagged branches are particularly common in landscape paintings of the fourteenth century. They are not so much trees, as forms of Far Eastern origin conceived in decorative terms. But landscapes from this period have come down to us in which the representation of trees shows real observation of nature. The most convincing examples are found in illustrations from the middle of the fourteenth century accompanying works of light literature. The distribution of branches and twigs and the shapes of their leaves, flowers and fruit, make these trees immediately recognisable not only in their

51 Hunting Scene

52 Fabulous Beasts

general kind but in their species. Shrubs, flowers and bushes are likewise naturalistically drawn in these
15 pictures, and the tufts of grass arranged in parallel rows give an impression of depth and distance in space.

Though atmospheric manifestations are represented quite naturalistically in the landscape paintings, the
rendering of water is stylized. It consists of lines of waves brought to life by an ornamentation of spirals and
rosettes. The masses of plastic whorls from the Chinese 'thundercloud' motif occur very often in these pictures. Yet, this stylized manner of representation is abandoned, in one or two instances, for a naturalistic
one in which the clouds, like veins in marble, form elliptical, elongated or oval bands.

Mongol landscape painting, in spite of its advanced naturalism, is not quite free of time-honoured pictorial
49 symbols, as may be seen from the representation of gnarled trees, spongy rocks and spirals of water and clouds.
But these stylized and borrowed forms are endowed with a new feeling for nature, and personal observation;
the abstractly decorative and the space-filling components are fused into the peculiar synthesis that is so
distinctive of the Chinese-Mongol trend in art.

In the Saray albums there is, besides these landscapes, a large quantity of Mongol drawings which, it must
be admitted, are not of the same quality. Beside the original we find copies, beside the master the pupils. A

series of these pictures is signed and several of these partially legible names are discussed by E. Kühnel in a paper.[124] Most of the signatures, however, are ascriptions from a later period. Since the anonymity of works of art in the east makes it hard to establish which signatures the artist would have regarded as his own, these offer no sound basis for an exact dating. The pages also vary widely in technical execution, in artistic character and in purpose. Some are monochrome, others polychrome, done with pen or brush; often they are covered with a wash or picked out in gold, or are in the nature of sketches, studies, mould-designs for book bindings, drawings in the margin, or the like.

These drawings include a group from the milieu of Mongol knights and courtiers as embodied in the pleasures of hunting and gaming, and representations from the end of the fourteenth century of very various *51* subjects (garden-scenes, rocky mountain-landscapes and the like), which by virtue of the subtle quality of the drawing clearly point the way from the Jala'irid to the Timurid style.[125]

An extensive collection of decorative drawings of an East Asian stamp also deserves mention; these are boldly executed with the paint brush, and with the organic rhythm of their line are the exact opposite of the abstract arabesque in character. Among these we find a series of motifs which were originally derived *52*

53   Animal Combat

93

54 Hyaenas

from the Far East. They include such things as the phoenix, the dragon, the lion and the stag *kilin* (unicorn) and, along with many decorative elements of landscape, the Mongol knot as well as the scarves blowing
33, 39 in the wind, the kerchiefs and fluttering ribbons that we find everywhere as decorative accessories in the works of Mongol painting.

The drawings of animals on the other hand achieve a fusion of the Near Eastern tradition of imagery with the influence of the Far East. The likeness to nature in these pages often produces an astounding effect. But the animal drawings shaped with so much realism do not originate from any personal observation of nature, but show forth the distinctive features in the movement of each animal species, such as the flight of the stag,
53, 54 the slink of the fox, or the attack of the leopard, which have been handed down for generations by a naturalistic tradition of imagery in the Far East.

In these drawings the contribution of the individual artist comes out above all in the particular manner in which the relevant forms are rendered. Owing to the strong attachment to tradition, a perfection of execution is achieved that can hardly be excelled. But traditionalism can also lead to a paralysis of the creative powers, and virtuosity can easily sink into routine. If most of the drawings of the fourteenth century avoid such a danger, they do it only because they belong to a living tradition. The artists indeed submit to the tradition, but at the same time they lend it new strength and new freshness.

The motifs, which are rendered again and again by innumerable hands, are not lifeless schemata but forms which derive from living experience. Hence even the copy has a new meaning here, and repetition has the significance of a new creation. This situation does not change until the fifteenth century, when artistic life begins to be dominated by a purely decorative tradition emptied of its human content and its historical significance.

POSTSCRIPT

In this book we have learned to know a manner of painting which still retains an essential element of the original power of the image and is thus clearly marked off from the decorative taste of Islamic miniatures. It is a style that remains under the spell of a cultural tradition native to Central Asia, in which the image, in sharp contrast to Islam, enjoys the highest recognition.

Mani's reputation as a painter still survives in the oral tradition of the east, and tradition asserts that Manichaeism owed its propagation in Central Asia above all to the persuasive power of the brush, which was used with masterly skill by the adherents of this religion. The truth of this tradition is attested by the paintings in books, and by murals done in the Manichaean monasteries of East Turkestan, which were the product of deep religious feeling, and should be placed at least on a level with their religious texts.

It was different in the west, in Iran and neighbouring countries, which with the Arab invasions fell from the seventh century onward within the sphere of Islam. According to this religion, divine truth was revealed in the word of the Koran, and the image, scorned and from time to time persecuted, could maintain itself only on the periphery of the spiritual world. This explains why a highly developed literature arose in the Islamic world, but no painting that could bear comparison with the works of this literature.

Painting of such a quality was brought to these lands by the Mongols, who, as heirs of the former Uighur Empire, carried westward the great pictorial tradition of Central Asia. The new language of forms from the east must at first have caused an indignant astonishment; but when the *Shahname*, the national epic of Persia, three centuries after its creation, took pictorial form before the eyes of the Mohammedans, that must have broken the ice, and painting gained so greatly in importance that, as may be seen from the representation of Mohammed's Ascension, it even ventured to give visible form to religious themes.

The penetration of the image into the world of Islam is a fundamental process in the history of the east, and it is Mongol painting that marks its course. The term 'Mongol' might give occasion for some objections. Why the emphasis on what is Mongol? Did not most of the works reproduced in this book originate on the ancient territory of Persian culture and had not that culture an essential part in their origin? Certainly the Mongols were the heirs of the Uighur Empire; they were the bearers of the eastern tradition of imagery to the west. But the subjugation of the Uighurs meant, as von Le Coq says, 'the dissolving of the Mongol national character in the Turkish world'. The Uighurs did indeed succumb to the overwhelming power of their eastern neighbours, but the conquerors on their side yielded to the superior culture of the former. The Mongols had no script of their own; they took it over from the Uighurs. Uighur secretaries and administrators presided over all business in the Mongol Empire that required higher education. It was the same in artistic life, where Uighur masters were everywhere in demand, and were always allowed to enjoy a privileged position at the court of the Mongol Great Khans and in the lands that they occupied. Should the Mongols, this nomad people of the steppes, which by its plundering expeditions and ruthless butchering of civilized peoples had made itself feared and hated, be called the bearers of a tradition of painting, which after all was on its side a product of many, often mutually opposed influences, and in which not only Manichee-Uighur art, but Sassanid and Chinese, Gandhara and other ancient sources of imagery also had a share?

Such questions certainly have their justification. Asia was from the earliest time a theatre for the great migrations of peoples, and the historian must take into account the mutual influences of different streams of culture, which in creative periods crystallized stylistic trends into great syntheses. Mongol painting was such a synthesis; an imperial art which arose in the crucible of the greatest world-empire in history and combined into a unity the cultural values of the Near and of the Far East.

The Mongol contribution is none the less of great importance and should not be underestimated, still less overlooked. The pages by the Siyah Qalem group that have come down to us (Ills. 27–47), and are now in the Topkapu Museum, have opened up for us the world of Mongol art at a time before this had developed into an imperial art. We are dealing with an art which stands in sovereign independence of the west and deserves to be called Central Asian in the most proper sense. That these pages, dating from as late as about 1400, were able to preserve their distinctively Mongol character is explained by their having originated at some distance from the leading centres of western Asian culture in the territory now known as Turkestan. Revealing as they do a hitherto unknown aspect of the world of the steppes, and its art, they may be counted one of the most distinctive creations of the Turco-Mongol nomad tribes of Inner Asia, who played a leading part in Asian history during the thirteenth and fourteenth centuries. The peculiar intensity of their manner, the dynamism and radiant energy that emanates from this barbarian art enables us to see how the Mongol conquerors could become 'bearers of culture' and appear as such in the west. History relates how Islamic culture fell a victim to the Mongols, and in this context it is forgotten that even before the Mongol conquest it had exhausted its possibilities of development and was bound to suffer an inner collapse as well before the superior power of the eastern cultures. The primeval vigour of the 'Mongol style' must surely have meant a rejuvenation for the over-refined and tired cultures of the Near East, which quickly fell under its spell.

Much that was once part of Mongol painting was later unmercifully destroyed by the iconoclastic trends in Islam. The picture of Mongol painting that we have tried to reconstruct in this book therefore remains a torso; but it does show the history of oriental painting in a different light from that in which we are accustomed to see it.

NOTES ON THE ILLUSTRATIONS

HEROIC LOVE

Illustrations to the MS of the poem 'Warqa wa Gulshah'

1 WARQA AND GULSHAH (7.2 × 17.7 cm.). MS of the poem *Warqa wa Gulshah*, first half of the 13th century, Istanbul, Topkapu Saray Museum, Hazine 841, p. 336.
A few plants and birds indicate a garden of dreams in which the two lovers meet. Their heads are framed in an aureole, which is of Far Eastern origin and is quite usual in Buddhist art as a sign of majesty and power. In Islamic miniature-painting the nimbus loses its original significance and serves rather formal and decorative purposes by effectively separating the head from its background in the picture.

2 DUEL (6.0 × 17.7 cm.). MS of the poem *Warqa wa Gulshah*, first half of the 13th century, Istanbul, Topkapu Saray Museum, Hazine 841, p. 22a.
In open fight Gulshah kills her lover's rival by piercing him in the back with her lance. The subject of Warqa and Gulshah is not the platonic but the epic form of love. The composition of the scene is determined by the direction in which the figures are moving, from right to left against the blue background, in accord with the gold-glinting lettering; the lance in Gulshah's hand points in this direction too.
Not only line but colour also is used in Islamic miniature-painting to obtain abstract effects. Colour, which in the small format of book-illustrations is both the decorative element and the one that brings out the individual motifs, can be used as a means of removing the appearance of reality from objects and lending them transparency; the colour-scale of this miniature, with its unreal lighting, is a unique example of this.

HEROIC EPIC

Illustrations to Fidausi's Shahname

3 ISFANDIYAR'S FIGHT WITH THE DRAGON (12.0 × 25.5 cm.). *Shahname* MS, 1330. Istanbul, Topkapu Saray Museum, Hazine 1479, p. 145a.
The heroes of the *Book of Kings* are giants who are endowed with demonic powers and perform wonders. Among their enemies are dragons and fabulous creatures, which give the illustrator the opportunity to create bold ornamental works.

4 ISFANDIYAR'S FIGHT WITH THE SIMURGH (11.0 × 22.5 cm.). *Shahname* MS, 1330. Istanbul, Topkapu Saray Museum, Hazine 1479, p. 145a.
As a motif the simurgh bird provides superb opportunities for ornamentation in illustrations to the *Shahname*. The fight between the aggressive bird and the hero takes place in a fantastic landscape, which has only occasional contacts with reality.

5 THE FOUR FAITHFUL COMPANIONS OF KAI KHUSRAU (13.0 × 22.5 cm.). *Shahname* MS, 1330. Istanbul, Topkapu Saray Museum, Hazine 1479, p. 125a.
The four loyal companions of Kai Khusrau meet their death in the mountains. The heroic figures are variations of a main ornamental motif, among whose elements are the flower-pattern on the clothes, the interlacing of the chain mail and the mask-like faces. The stylised mountain peaks, shining with improbable colours, betoken a mythical landscape which belongs to the *Shahname* alone.

6 THE BIRTH OF RUSTAM (8.0 × 19.4 cm.). *Shahname* MS, beginning of the 14th century. Stiftung Preussischer Kulturbesitz, Tübinger Depot der Staatsbibliothek. Diez A. Fol. 71, p. 79.

In the *Shahname* the national hero of Persia is often compared with a lion or an elephant on account of his vigour and strength. Because he was already too large in the womb, his birth required a Caesarian section. In this hour of peril, the mythical bird, the Simurgh, appears to Zal, Rustam's father and gives him a feather which is to heal the wound of Rudabe his mother. It is characteristic of the narrative mode of representation that here two different episodes of the legend are shown on the same illustrated strip; on the right in the centre of a group is the half-lying gigantic, Cybele-like form of a woman, only partly covered with a blue patterned cloth, who supports herself in the pain of a difficult birth with out-stretched arms on two women appearing minutely small in comparison with her. The scene on the left is separated from this by a curtain. In front of a hearth, on which something is burning in an open container, Rustam's father crouches with one knee drawn up and receives a feather from the Simurgh, who far exceeds Zal in size. Both the index finger of the raised right hand and the flat outstretched palm of the left, are speaking gestures and signify a conversation.

7 PRINCE SIYAWUSH'S ORDEAL BY FIRE (8.0 × 19.4 cm.). *Shahname* MS, beginning of the 14th century. Stiftung Preussischer Kulturbesitz. Tübinger Depot der Staatsbibliothek. Diez A. Fol. 71, p 30.

To prove his innocence, the unfortunate Prince Siyawush has to ride through a pile of burning faggots. He appears in the picture, as in the text, on his 'night-coloured' charger Shabrang 'in white costume and golden helmet'. On the left in front of the stylized fortress two men, astonished at the event, raise their folded hands to heaven. On the very surface of the wall the king's head is to be seen as he watches the unusual event from the fortress.

WAR PICTURES

Illustrations to Rashid-ed-Din's World Chronicle

8 THE CAPTURE OF A TOWN (37.2 × 29.0 cm.). *Jami-et-Tawarikh* MS, beginning of the 14th century. Stiftung Preussischer Kulturbesitz, Tübinger Depot der Staatsbibliothek. Diez A. Fol. 71, p. 7.

On a bridge of boats, fastened to the banks with heavy chains and reaching from a great gate across the river to the fortress walls on the opposite side, stands the Commander-in-Chief, sceptre in hand, with his attendant. Both are watching a battle which is taking place in the foreground before their eyes. A number of archers can be seen in fighting attitude on the walls. Under the protection of shields, set close to one another in a row, they form three groups of three men each. In the left foreground, on the edge of the picture, stands a great ballista served by two men. Another ballista stands to the right on top of the wall.

Only one of the opposing sides is represented; their opponents are missing. Is this a siege or is it the defence of a town? From the picture it is hard to tell. A few characteristic features of the scenery remind one of the topography of Baghdad, which is divided by the Tigris into two parts. If this is really a picture of Baghdad, the town's conquest by the Mongols might be its subject.

9 STAMPEDED HORSES (24.4 × 26.1 cm.). *Jami-et-Tawarikh* MS, beginning of the 14th century. Stiftung Preussischer Kulturbesitz. Tübinger Depot der Staatsbibliothek. Diez A. Fol. 70, p. 19, top.

Horses are seen rushing towards each other. The main subject of representation is the animals; the human figures are only accessory. The group of sharply overlapping warriors at the right-hand edge of the picture is drawn so faintly in light brushwork that one at first overlooks them. One single warrior stands on the left, and high on top of a wall the row of archers taking aim is seen as a narrow band on the upper edge of the page.

In this frame, enclosed on three sides, horses, stampeded as an advance guard, rush at one another under a hail of arrows. Some look back over their shoulders; most of them gallop with lowered heads against the enemy without looking at him. The blind bestial force unleashed here threatens to discharge itself at the first shock of meeting and to trample down everything that stands in its way. A tremendous dynamism pours forth from this picture, where everything shares in the over-all movement occasioned by the turmoil of battle.

10 CAVALRY PURSUIT (7.0 × 24.0 cm.). *Jami-et Tawarikh* MS, 1314. Istanbul, Topkapu Saray Museum, Hazine 1653, p. 165b.

Warriors and riders, pressed into iron coats of mail with their heads drawn down deep between the shoulders and riding on 'flying' horses, form two bunched-up groups, which make contact in the middle of the picture. The foremost rider of the pursuing group tries with sabre in hand to reach the man in front of him, while the attitude of the fugitive's head and body is one of recoil from the pursuer. Everything in this scene, dominated by diagonals, is caught up in a forward-thrusting movement. Whirls of dust and cloud, the overlapping of the frame at the sides, a dropped lance and some parts of bodies under the horses' feet support this movement, which propagates itself with uncanny speed in this illustrated strip.

To cram as many fast-moving figures as possible into a narrow space is a technique used by the Mongol artist to heighten to the utmost the effect of the scene he depicts—which here threatens to burst out of its frame.

THE RULER'S PICTURE AS A SYMBOL OF POWER

11 A RULER ENTHRONED (37.0 × 26.2 cm.). Saray Album, about 1300. Istanbul, Topkapu Saray Museum, Hazine 2152, p. 60b.

The scene occupies two facing pages. On the left is the picture of a Mongol prince seated in ceremonial attitude in the midst of his retinue of state; the right-hand page (here reproduced as a sketch) shows a triumphal procession, directed toward the ruler, in which riders with hunting hawks and various animals and fabulous creatures take part as an act of homage. In the Near East the ruler's image is a symbol of power, as is indicated by the throne, the aureole round the royal head, the angel figures crowning the ruler, the triumphal procession, and the goblet in the king's hand.

These pages are the first two, that is, the frontispiece pages, of a lost manuscript.

12 GAYUMART, THE FIRST KING, IN THE MOUNTAINS (20.0 × 20.0 cm.). *Shahname* MS, middle of the 14th century. Istanbul, Topkapu Saray Museum, Hazine 2153, p. 55b.

The ceremonial picture of the ruler is here transformed into a naturalistically rendered scene. The only iconographical elements which can still be explained as symbols of power and strength are, apart from the panther-skin surcoats of the ruler and his attendants, the alarming beasts at their feet; heraldic versions of there are, however, to be found on frontispieces of the pre-Mongol period.

11. A ruler enthroned

99

13 VISIT TO THE HERMIT (20.1 × 27.4 cm.). Saray-album, middle of the 14th century. Stiftung Preussischer Kulturbesitz. Tübinger Depot der Staatsbibliothek. Diez A. Fol. 71, p. 2.

The scene takes place, surrounded by the loneliness of nature, in a grotto, which in contrast to its dark surroundings is flooded with light. In this rarefied atmosphere two men are in conversation: on the left is the crouching figure of a white-bearded anchorite with long hair, his withered arms and legs emerging from ragged clothes; opposite him, in the humble attitude of a visitor, sits the king with folded arms, half kneeling at the entrance of the grotto, and reverently holding his right hand at his breast.

The picture illustrates a legendary story, which is to be found in several manuscripts under various titles (Alexander and Diogenes, Khusrau Parviz and the Anchorite, etc.) Our miniature is among the earliest representations in this series. Though the scene is depicted with many contrasts, the execution is simple and avoids all decorative additions. The scenery here consists of a wall of rock overgrown with wild shrubs, on the right of which a grazing deer and two mules are to be seen.

14 THE SEVEN SLEEPERS (29.0 × 29.5 cm.). Saray-album, toward the end of the 14th century. Istanbul, Topkapu Saray Museum, Hazine 2160, p. 83a.

The Mongols seem to have taken pleasure in this legend. We encounter the theme first in the illustrations to the World Chronicle of Rashid-ed-Din and later in several of the stock of albums in the Saray Library.

As in the legend, the Seven Sleepers with the dog Kitmir are in a grotto, which is indicated by the round outline within which the group is very skilfully arranged. The picture might be regarded as a group portrait. The postures of the sitting and reclining sleepers have nothing stylized about them, and the artist's personal observation plays a great part in the rendering. The individual physiognomies, in spite of the closed eyes, differ markedly from one another and show genuine traits of portraiture, which are set forth with humour to most convincing effect.

15 THE MAN AMONG THE MONKEYS (24.0 × 25.0 cm.). Saray album, second half of the 14th century. Istanbul, Topkapu Saray Museum, Hazine 2153, p. 155b.

Four monkeys are climbing down from trees and surrounding a white-bearded man, who wears a great ornamental turban on his head and a leather belt adorned with silver around his waist. In his right hand he holds a club in threatening fashion over his shoulder, as he looks sideways at one of the monkeys, which approaches close to him.

Gnarled trees with serrated and intertwined branches, abundant foliage, and pomegranate trees laden with fruit render the surrounding landscape. A few rows of grasses and plants give the ground, from which an outcrop of rock sticks up, a positively furrowed appearance.

The picture represents an episode from a story that deals with the peculiar adventure of a man with a female monkey. On another page the same man's meeting with the devil is represented (Hazine 2153, p. 12a). Two further episodes of the story are to be found in the Berlin Saray Albums (Diez A. Fol. 71, p. 12 and Diez A. Fol. 72, p. 19).

16 FIGHT IN A BOAT (19.5 × 28.8 cm.). Saray album, second half of the 14th century. Istanbul, Topkapu Saray Museum, Hazine 2153, p. 107a.

In a black boat out at sea four young mullas are engaged in a life-and-death struggle. They wear the simple dress of their office and tightly-wound turbans. Immediately in front of the boat we see another man, who was presumably thrown overboard, struggling in the water; only his head and lacquered boots are still to be seen above the surface. The drowning man's turban has been carried away by the waves. A man is rowing to the scene of action in a small boat, abruptly cut off by the edge of the picture.

17 BATTLE OF THE CROWS AND THE OWLS (19.8 × 17.2 cm.). *Kalila and Dimna MS*, 1370. Istanbul University Library F. 1422, p. 7b.

Behind this picture is a story from *Kalila and Dimna*. With their wings the crows are fanning a fire, in which they are burning to death their enemies, the owls. We see the flames blazing and the crows flying up against the steep mountain-side; the owls which are crowded into a hole in the rock can be made out only with difficulty. This makes it harder to understand the story, which for the artist was no more than the occasion for painting a landscape. The method of presentation of the earlier *Kalila and*

Dimna illustrations was narrative; here it is descriptive. Compare this page with the representation of the same scene in the *Kalila and Dimna* illustrations 1200–1220 in the Bibliothèque Nationale, Paris, Arabic MS 3467, Folio 78 verso).

18 THE DONKEY AND THE JACKAL (11.2 × 19.0 cm.). *Kalila and Dimna* MS, 1370. Istanbul, University Library F. 1422, p. 11a.
The scenery of the picture consists of a screen of rock and a bent tree in the background. The donkey and the jackal seem to be involved in an exciting conversation. The animals in *Kalila and Dimna* have the gift of speech; here, in addition, their physiognomies show human traits.

The artist paints his animals from close at hand. The close view leads to a narrowing of the field of vision. The resulting impression as of a section of a larger picture is only strengthened by the way in which the lateral edges look as though they had been trimmed, and by partial framing inside the picture itself.
The setting is made to suit the main figures of the fable. It takes up something of the rhythm of the figures and in turn relates them to the background. The drawing, which applies crude outlines and contrasted shading to the rocks, takes on in the animal representations a refined and differentiated structure, so that even the bristly skin of the donkey is distinguished from the soft skin of the jackal.

RELIGIOUS PAINTING AND EARLY REPRESENTATIONS OF HEAVEN
The Master Ahmed Musa

19 THE PROPHET WITH THE ARCHANGEL GABRIEL IN HEAVEN (28.0 × 24.0 cm.). Ascension of Mohammed, second quarter of the 14th century. Istanbul, Topkapu Saray Museum, Hazine 2154, p. 31b.
Hosts of angels receive the Prophet on his Ascension. To judge by their spread wings, the angels are only just arriving on the scene and have not yet had time to range themselves before him. The subject is the unexpected moment of meeting.

The Prophet stands on the extreme right-hand edge of the picture, with the Archangel Gabriel who accompanies him on his journey. He is the beholder and narrator, through whose agency we are enabled to share in the wonderful events that take place before his eyes in Heaven. But here the wonder is observed and depicted with human eyes. There is nothing about the angelic forms, except their wings and Sassanid crowns, to suggest that they are transcendental beings. Their solid build gives the divine envoys an earthbound character, and the Mongol dress with its short-sleeved surcoat corresponds exactly to the fashion that prevailed in the fourteenth century in countries occupied by the Mongols. The artist is obviously concerned in the first place with a convincing representation of the legend. The Prophet's vision is rendered in the picture as an event in space and time; in fact the giant figure of the angel in the foreground breaks in upon the rows of angels behind to such an extent that the picture gives the impression of depth in space. The Prophet's head is surrounded by a nimbus of flames. The veil before his face was painted on at a later date.

20 THE HEAVENLY COCK (31.2 × 24.0 cm.). *Mi'rajname* MS, second quarter of the 14th century. Istanbul, Topkapu Saray Museum, Hazine 2154, p. 61b.
Here the giant figure of a cock enthroned on a high stool, gleaming white against the dark silver of the background, positively draws the eye to him. Drawn up in ranks before the throne, angelic hosts worship him. Their hands raised in prayer and their heads stretching upwards are directed toward him. Even the archangel in the right of the picture points to the cock, while the Prophet beside him remains still in the animal's presence and holds his hands reverently folded before his breast.

21 MOHAMMED ABOVE THE MOUNTAINS (35.5 × 24.5 cm.). *Mi'rajname* MS, second quarter of the 14th century. Istanbul, Topkapu Saray Museum, Hazine 2154, p. 42b.
Gabriel, accompanied by a host of lesser angels, carries the Prophet over the mountains. A fine graining transmutes the golden ground of the picture, which suggests the glow of heaven *(hvarenah)*, into an atmosphere flooded with light, and the white mountain peaks and individual figures of angels rise up as if from a blazing sea of flame. The flying, resting or standing figures of angels are represented in naturalistic fashion.

22 THE PROPHET ABOVE THE WATER (18.0 × 24.0 cm.). *Mi'rajname* MS, second quarter of the 14th century. Istanbul, Topkapu Saray Museum, Hazine 2154, p. 121a.

The Archangel carries the Prophet over the water, which is rendered by parallel wavy lines and spirals. Here too the Prophet is carried on the angel's shoulders. The picture is the only one among our representations of the Ascension in which the nocturnal flight of Mohammed takes place in complete solitude.

23 PRESENTATION OF A TOWN (35.7 × 25.3 cm.). *Mi'rajname* MS, second quarter of the 14th century. Istanbul, Topkapu Saray Museum, Hazine 2154, p. 107a.

Halfway up the page, on the left, sits Mohammed (?) in a flaming *mandorla* on a carpet patterned in geometric motifs. His raised right hand (a speaking gesture) shows that he is addressing the two figures who kneel in a reverent attitude facing him in front of the carpet. Above them hovers a crowned angelic figure with outspread wings and offers to the principal character seated on the carpet the model of a town divided by a river into two parts. The minarets in the modelled town are a Turkish feature. The assumption that this may be intended to represent the later capital of Islam on the Golden Horn gains further support by the blue waterway. Below this scene is a row of seated figures which are turned toward the principal character and arranged in smaller groups. The two standing figures at the bottom right-hand corner appear to be acting as mediators or narrators for the benefit of the spectator.

The landscape in which the scene takes place is rendered with a few masses of rock, plant-motifs and tufts of grass set at irregular intervals.

24 THE ASCENSION OF MOHAMMED (31.5 × 48.0 cm.). *Mi'rajname* MS, ca. 1350. Istanbul, Topkapu Saray Museum, Hazine 2154, p. 68b.

In accordance with widespread tradition of his Ascension, Mohammed embarks on his flight on the fabulous beast, Burak. He is shown with the body of a winged horse and has a human head. In this picture the earth far below is rendered with a few clusters of leaves, scattered standing shrubs and a pond. High above the earth floats Mohammed, accompanied by four angels, on the back of Burak. His head is surrounded with an aureole, like those of the angels. Behind the Prophet is a magnificent cloud motif, a dense, rotating, wind-borne shape whose indented edges give it the form of a blazing flame. Bright bodies terminate below in two ends narrowing to a point, which blow in the wind like banners.

25 ABRAHAM'S SACRIFICE (32.8 × 48.3 cm.). Saray album, toward the end of the 14th century. Istanbul, Topkapu Saray Museum, Hazine 2154, p. 119a.

The scene is laid in a bare mountain landscape between great masses of rock which fill the picture up to the top. The figures wear Mongol dress. In spite of the spreading wings, the crowned angel who brings the sacrificial animal looks like someone racing to the spot rather than sweeping down in flight. The attitude of Abraham, as he kneels upon the ground, goes back to ancient sacrificial gestures. Holding his drawn dagger to the neck of the youth as he lies upon the ground, he turns his head towards the angel.

26 AN ANGEL CARRIES OFF A YOUNG PRINCE (49.0 × 35.5 cm.). Saray Album, end of the 14th century. Istanbul, Topkapu Saray Museum, Hazine 2152, p. 69a.

Descending in a tremendous swoop, an angel seizes a young Prince, clasps him and carries him away from the earth. The Prince is characterised by his crown and tiraz bands with their inscription *as-Sultan al-Malik* 'the Sultan, the King'. The landscape shows decorative accessories and already foreshadows the stylistic peculiarities of Timurid art.

PICTURES OF DEMONS AND SCENES FROM THE LIFE OF THE NOMADS

27 THE ANGELS' BATTLE WITH THE DRAGONS (27.5 × 37.0 cm.). Saray album early 15th century. Istanbul, Topkapu Saray Museum, Hazine 2153, p. 5b. This magnificent battle-scene in which six angels bind the dragons in the abyss, belongs in its iconographical content to the world of Buddhist belief. The powerful figures of the angels fighting on the wing are closely akin to the angelic figures of Ahmed Musa. They wear fluttering baggy garments and their bell shaped hair-style with a plait at the crown

corresponds to the fashion of the pre-Timurid age. The rock formations, variously aligned, are, to judge from their structure, of a rough, porous texture. They are more like a layer of bark than any kind of stone. The scanty growth of plants consists of a tree-stump and a few leaves. The dragons' bodies writhing between the rocks are represented in the naturalistic style of the end of the fourteenth century.

28 ILLUSTRATION TO AN EAST ASIAN FOLKTALE (20.5 × 31.5 cm.). Saray album, 14th century. Istanbul, Topkapu Saray Museum, Hazine 2153, p. 165a.
The Saray albums include a series of illustrations to an East Asiatic folktale, which once formed a roll. Torn out of this roll, they now make a bundle of loose pages, to which the illustration reproduced here belongs. It represents two demons in hasty flight, carrying two treasure-chests under their arms. One of the demons has peculiar wings in the form of a pair of stag's antlers.

29 DONKEY WITH TWO DEMONS (27.0 × 36.0 cm.). Saray album, 14th century. Istanbul, Topkapu Saray Museum, Hazine 2153, p. 27b.

30 TWO DEMON MUSICIANS (15.6 × 33.2 cm.). Saray album, 14th century. Istanbul, Topkapu Saray Museum, Hazine 2153, p. 112a.
The pictures of dancing and music-making demons of the desert in illustrations 30 and 33 recall a passage in Marco Polo's *Travels* (Yule-Cordier, vol. I, p. 197) which mentions the spirits of the great desert beyond the city of Lop, that is, the south-western Gobi. 'Even in the day-time one hears those spirits talking. And sometimes you shall hear the sound of a variety of musical instruments, and still more commonly the sound of drums.' The accompanying notes give other examples of such beliefs and mention the noises in deserts that suggest them.

31 DEMON CARRYING OFF A HORSE (20.5 × 16.5 cm.). Saray album, 14th century. Istanbul, Topkapu Saray Museum, Hazine 2153, p. 38a.
A number of pictures in the Saray albums give us information on the religious ideas of the Mongols in their pre-Islamic period. The principal figures in these pages are demons, which may be described as peculiar hybrid creatures. They are distinguished from human beings by their horns, tails, skins, their terrifying masks of faces and still other animal-demonic attributes which are superimposed like a mask on their solidly built human bodies. In any case these monsters are very like human beings and make the gestures of human beings: they hold an emaciated donkey, play musical instruments, carry off horses, struggle and dance like human beings and sacrifice a horse in a ritual act for an unknown god. Even their clothing is like human clothing: they wear aprons and gold rings round their necks and on their hands and feet. Their muscles are always bursting with strength, no less in rest than in fighting. Whether they sit or stand, converse or lift enormous weights, their bodies are always tense and in motion and they are always ready to leap up and to exercise their limbs. A few demons' figures actually recall the fantastic creations of Gothic. But while in the Christian world these were regarded as symbols of the negative powers, here they seem to spring from a heathen world of ideas, which does not yet know a duality of heaven and earth, which makes demons of the secret powers of nature, and at the same time tries to exercise them. Perhaps these pictures are meant to be personifications of such natural powers, and it is not impossible that we have shamans here, who mimic demons with bizarre masks and in grotesque animal shapes, and thus try to exorcise them so as to heal man and beast.

32 HORSE SACRIFICE (19.5 × 49.5 cm.). Saray album, 14th century. Istanbul, Topkapu Saray Museum, Hazine 2153, p. 40b.
This picture represents a ritual act, in which the participants dismember a white horse and swing its limbs, still dripping with blood, round themselves like scarves. To the left behind a hill two truncated onlookers are visible in torso. We see only their heads and a hand silhouetted against the light, turned toward us in a warning gesture. In the left-hand bottom corner of the picture a demon figure is about to bring down a horse's haunch in a two-handed blow upon a crouching figure, while the latter like a petrified symbol of apprehension and horror tries to protect himself by warding it off with his hands. In this grisly picture of frenzy carried to the point of madness, ecstasy reaches its climax.

33 DANCING DEMONS (22.5 × 48.0 cm.). Saray album, 14th century. Istanbul, Topkapu Saray Museum, Hazine 2153, p. 64b.
This ecstatic picture of demons dancing likewise belongs to this group of cult-scenes. The painter

shows himself a master of rhythmic movement. As if obsessed by the aspect of the feet, he becomes one with the dance of the figures that he draws. The movement is presented in sequence. It is divided into different phases, succeeding one another in time and arranged in a whirligig montage, so that before our eyes everything passes into indescribable movement. Arms and feet, bodies and flying scarves are whirled round as by a cyclone.

34 THE FIGHT WITH THE DEMON (18.0 × 23.5 cm.). Saray album, 14th century. Istanbul, Topkapu Saray Museum, Hazine 2153, p. 64a.
The hero's fight with the demon is one of the favourite themes of eastern epics. With all his might the giant is dashed to the ground by the man. An unusual picture by the master Siyah Qalem, in which nature, in the form of a tree, is also represented. With its roots reaching deep into the ground, its mutilated branches, withered leaves, horny bark and trunk sawn through, so that the age-rings are visible, the tree here is a symbol of nature in its phases of life. It repeats the rhythm of the figures struggling in the foreground and thereby intensifies their movement.

35 GIANT SUPPORTING HIMSELF ON A STAFF (18.0 × 23.5 cm.). Saray album, 14th century. Istanbul, Topkapu Saray Museum, Hazine 2153, p. 23a.
This silhouetted figure on a white ground reminds us of a shadow-play. The gigantic figure, who twines one leg firmly round the staff and balances on one foot, light as a feather, could be one of such a play's chief characters, cut out of leather and moved behind the curtain. The shadow here is not dully flat. It is touched with life by the coloured reflection of light, and gains a transparency that enables us to see the body clearly in its anatomy.

36 QUARRY (16.5 × 26.5 cm.). Saray album, 14th century. Istanbul, Topkapu Saray Museum, Hazine 2153, p. 105a.
On the right is a man felled to the ground by a rock that has landed on his head. He lies prone on the ground like one struck by lightning, his legs twisted, whitle his turban rolls away from him. His companion, petrified at the sight of this accident, bites the index finger of his left hand and holds his head with his right – a typical gesture of amazement often found in the east, both in pictures and in life. A few fragments of rock strewn over the plane of the picture suggest the scene's setting.

37 CONVERSATION SCENE (12.0 × 17.3 cm.). Saray album, 14th century. Istanbul, Topkapu Saray Museum, Hazine 2153, p. 140a.
Here too we have a representation which is so like a scene from a shadow-play that it might be taken for one. This impression is particularly brought home by the nature of the scene and by the rendering of the figures, which appear as dark shadows on the light plane of the picture as if they had been cut out with scissors. The entire expressive power of the line is concentrated in the sharp edges which arrest the attention of the spectator. But thanks to a very deliberate and mannered lighting the inner shapes are no less important than the outlines. The figures are lit from within by a variable glimmering light which in places breaks up the dense massive shadows and makes the anatomy of the body clearly visible. The bodies of these supply bent figures, which have clothes wound about their necks and arms, are neatlimbed and move their joints easily; even in the sitting position the figures seem to be balanced as in a dance.

38 THE CROUCHING GIANT (13.0 × 12.5 cm.). Saray album, 14th century. Istanbul, Topkapu Saray Museum, Hazine 2153, p. 28a.
The crouching form of this black giant is marked by a solid sculptural quality. The arms and feet, heavy and massive, are like living clubs into which the artist has compressed all the energy of the body. The legs open as if they wished to encompass the invisible but ever-present earth.

39 DANCING SHAMANS (18.5 × 25.0 cm.). Saray album, 14th century. Istanbul, Topkapu Saray Museum, Hazine 2153, p. 34b.
The black colossi leap about with elemental force, their bodies rebounding from the ground. The movement seems to begin in the figure that turns its back to us and to be continued in the convolutions of the figure facing us. This twisting action is very skilfully conveyed by the expressive dislocation of the limbs and particularly of the soles of the feet. Even the fluttering bands of cloth participate in the frenzied movement of the bodies. In contrast to the classical dance, the movement here does not seek to free the bodies from the ground, which is seen to draw them to itself, so that their weight is very

apparent. Everything has an earthward urge, and everything shoots upward from the earth. It is not harmony that is important here, but rhythm of movement. In accordance with this rhythm, the master divides the movements into single phases and brings them together in a montage which conveys the impression of a rhythmical dance.

40 STANDING MEN IN CONVERSATION (25.5 × 16.0 cm.). Saray album, 14th century. Istanbul, Topkapu Saray Museum, Hazine 2153 p. 38a.
Powerful old men play a chief part in Siyah Qalem's pictures. Again and again we encounter their majestic bearing and hard expression. If these bearded men lean on sticks, they seem like towers in their rocklike stability. They cleave so firmly to the earth that their whole strength seems to be derived from their weight. The build of these solid bodies is visible even under the flowing folds of their baggy clothing. Their muscles have exaggerated bulges and the very way they grip their traveller's staffs suggests a great elemental strength, which it seems to be the master's principal concern to express.

41 NOMAD FAMILY (14.0 × 25.0 cm.). Saray album, 14th century. Istanbul, Topkapu Saray Museum, Hazine 2153, p. 23b.
In Siyah Qalem's hard world this idyllic family scene is an exception, and shows that he was not lacking in a sense of humour. His observation of nature, which is expressed elsewhere in conventional form, takes on a certain personal note here, and we have the impression that this is a description of a scene from everyday life in camp. The old man, father of the family, is feeding the animal. One of the boys looks on with childish curiosity, the others press round their mother. With their clothes and headdresses, these people recall the nomads who can even today still be met in southern Anatolia.

42 NOMADS (14.0 × 26.0 cm.). Saray album, 14th century. Istanbul, Topkapu Saray Museum, Hazine 2153, p. 55a.
We see people who have been engaged all their lives in burdensome wandering on foot. Their feet are like misshapen paws and are as expressively depicted as their faces. The old man in the middle, offset by the black patch made by the donkey, forms a group with his two companions, and all three crowd close together. The left-hand figure of this central group,

skilfully linked with the figures on the sides, looks anxiously at the man who is carrying the invalid, but keeps close to his own group. The leader on the right, through the position of his arm, and his look, fits in with the group of walkers. The interconnection of the whole is further emphasized by the play of the men's looks, which are all directed toward the centre, thereby in some degree expressing the scheme of composition.
In spite of his great effort to hold the composition together, the painter does not succeed in overcoming his habit of showing everything individually in sequence. In fact the characters are ranged one after another on the same plane, and given equal prominence; their only endeavour, as on the stage, is not to cut off each other's view so that each one of them shall be clearly visible. This explains the painfully accurate representation of the many feet, of which not one is sacrificed for the sake of the whole.

43 NOMAD CAMP (19.5 × 37.0 cm.). Saray album, 14th century. Istanbul, Topkapu Saray Museum, Hazine 2153, p. 1b.
This picture too is one of the rare representations by Siyah Qalem in which the treatment is descriptive: two men in conversation are washing their clothes; the fire-blower is occupied with preparing the meal; grazing and playing animals, nomad weapons, saddles and pieces of leather equipment are rendered one next to the other. No doubt the master who painted this page is attempting to be as true to nature as possible. But his drawing is still not the direct result of observing nature: it is far removed from catching the everyday appearance of the things represented. We are presented with forms which have more or less the character of schematised memory-images. Some of these forms, such as the motif of the fire-blower or the pair of dogs at play, occur in other drawings of the Saray albums (Hazine 2153, p. 51b). The artist's personal contribution in this page is so much taken up with rendering traditional forms that we are no longer able to distinguish it in details.

44 A NOMAD LEADS HIS EMACIATED HORSE BY THE BRIDLE (13.5 × 25.0 cm.). Saray album, 14th century, ca. 1400. Istanbul, Topkapu Saray Museum, Hazine 2153, p. 118b.
Line, supported by shading which is rich in contrasts, is Siyah Qalem's typical means of expression. By this means he conveys with unsurpassable

realism the folds in the nomad's clothing, the mane and ribs of his horse. In this drawing too he has avoided rigidity in the movement of the walking animal; the horse's feet are represented in the same fashion as in the previous picture.

45 A NOMAD GRAZES HIS HORSE (16.2 × 25.5 cm.). Saray album, 14th century. Istanbul, Topkapu Saray Museum, Hazine 2153, p. 84a.
This picture offers us an impressively faithful likeness of a nomad grazing his horse. The grazing animal turns its head straight toward us; we see its mouth and nose from the side but its forehead from the front, while its muzzle is again shown from the side. This horse's head is as abstract in effect as a Picasso drawing. In spite of the obvious attempt to be true to nature, the painter has not restricted himself to a single viewing angle. This enables him to render movement in successive phases. The animal's feet, seen alternately from above and from below, likewise indicate that the artist is showing its walk and stride not simultaneously but in sequence.

46 A HORSE IS GROOMED (15.5 × 25.4 cm.). Saray album, ca. 1400. Istanbul, Topkapu Saray Museum, Hazine 2160, p. 50b.
A white-bearded negro disciplines with his riding whip a horse that is tied to the peg. The great rounded body of the animal writhing on its back on the ground is caught in movement in masterly fashion and its upward-straining head with wildly disarrayed mane is a brilliant example of an art whose main object is expressiveness. The picture comes from the circle of Siyah Qalem's school.

47 WARRIOR WITH HORSE (21.3 × 24.5 cm.). Saray album, ca. 1400. Istanbul.
The subject is a warrior who is about to plait the tail of his war-horse. Dark green foliage in the background and a few asters and clusters of leaves on the ground suffice for the setting. The warrior wears an ornate belt around his gold-studded blue cloak adorned with Chinese spiral patterns, and a golden helmet embellished with costly fur. The light-brown horse with its magnificent mane and streaked back stands looking over its shoulder. It is tethered to a peg by means of a strap from the bridle.
The picture, which is painted on silk, does not come from the immediate circle to which the works of Siyah Qalem belong, but nevertheless from a source sharing the same artistic trends. Here too influence of the Far East is undeniable, even though the total conception, plan and execution show a certain independence.

LANDSCAPE PAINTING, ANIMAL DRAWING

48 BIRD IN A ROCKY LANDSCAPE (33.0 × 46.5 cm.). Saray album, second half of the 14th century. Istanbul, Topkapu Saray Museum, Hazine 2153, p. 30a.
The painter of this page knows that by juxtaposing near-by objects and distant views in a picture he can create a particularly strong effect of depth. The bird in the foreground is presented in the closest proximity, so that even the feathers on its wings can be distinguished clearly. In contrast to this very large bird, the three trees in the middle distance are shown minutely small. Because of this offsetting in the picture, the crudely drawn masses of rock in the background retreat into the far distance and we have the impression of standing in a landscape surrounded by high mountains. The vastness of nature not only comes out in wide landscapes, but can be evoked by means of perspective even in a cut-out section. This play on perspective was much favoured by Mongol artists, as their many pictures of landscapes make plain.

49 SUMMER LANDSCAPE (32.5 × 42.5 cm.). Saray album, middle of the 14th century. Istanbul, Topkapu Saray Museum, Hazine 2153, p. 68a.
Perspective was used in Mongol landscape-painting of the 14th century. A case in point is this panorama-like bird's-eye view in which trees and mountains grow ever smaller the further the eye moves into the interior of the picture, thereby producing an impression of depth. The landscape in the middle distance, painted in pastel shades, exhibits a naturalistic *pointilliste* manner of painting. The water that gushes forth in the foreground, on the other hand, takes the form of stylized spiralling foam-patterns. Conversely, the traditional decorative spiral cloud-pattern is replaced by naturalistic multi-coloured cloud formations with an irregular marble-like quality. Received forms and personal observation, abstract-decorative elements and three-dimensional effects are combined into a peculiar synthesis which is characteristic of the Chinese-Mongol tradition of art.

50 ISKANDAR'S FIGHT WITH THE WOLVES (32.5 × 28.5 cm.). Saray album, 1370. Istanbul, Topkapu Saray Museum, Hazine 2153, p. 73b.

The picture relates to a story in the *Shahname* which tells of Iskandar's fight with fabulous creatures. But the artist has used the theme only as an occasion for depicting a mountain landscape overgrown with trees, which draws the attention of the spectator wholly to itself. The method of representation is adapted to the naturalistic-descriptive style of the second half of the 14th century.

51 HUNTING SCENE (18 × 27 cm.). Saray album, end of the 14th century. Istanbul, Topkapu Saray Museum, Hazine 2160, p. 84 a.

Four Mongol riders with hunting hawks and a dog move along a steep hill to the hunt. The diagonal arrangement of the figures, sharply cut off by the slope of the hill, sets up in the interior of the picture a line of movement which determines its con-figuration in space. In the foreground are a few flat masses of rock piled one upon the other, a leafless tree with jagged branches and two slain panthers. The manner in which the landscape and figures are drawn already reveals peculiarities of the Timurid style. The use of bright and contrasted hues reflects the differentiated and over-refined sense of colour in Mongol art about 1400.

52 FABULOUS BEASTS (26.0 × 37.7 cm.). Saray album, ca. 1400. Istanbul, Topkapu Saray Museum, Hazine 2153, p. 170b.

The Saray albums contain a comprehensive collection of decorative drawings of East Asian stamp, which with their organically activated rhythm of line have a character that is the direct opposite of abstract ara-besque. The motifs that occur in these drawings, such as the dragon, the Simurgh, the lion-*kilin* (unicorn), the stag-*kilin*, and other warring fabulous creatures, likewise indicate their Far Eastern origin. They were introduced from the Central Asian homeland of the Mongols and then passed into the general stock of Near Eastern imagery.

On this page, offset by some tree and cloud motifs, are two fabulous creatures facing one another; they have flaming wings on their breasts and legs and are shown with backward-facing heads and legs drawn up in flight. The creatures' movements unravelling themselves in different directions are adapted to the rhythm of the fluttering bands round their bodies.

53 ANIMAL COMBAT (14.5 × 25.5 cm.). Saray album ca. 1400. Istanbul, Topkapu Saray Museum, Hazine 2160, p. 90b.

54 HYAENAS (16.0 × 32.0 cm.). Saray album, ca. 1400. Istanbul, Topkapu Saray Museum, Hazine 2153, p. 19b.

This is a characteristic example of the fusion of the Near Eastern tradition of imagery with the influence of the Far East. The rendering of the hyaenas conveys the distinctive traits of these lithe animals, not however with a realism deriving from personal observation but by adapting the centuries-old naturalistic tradition of the Orient.

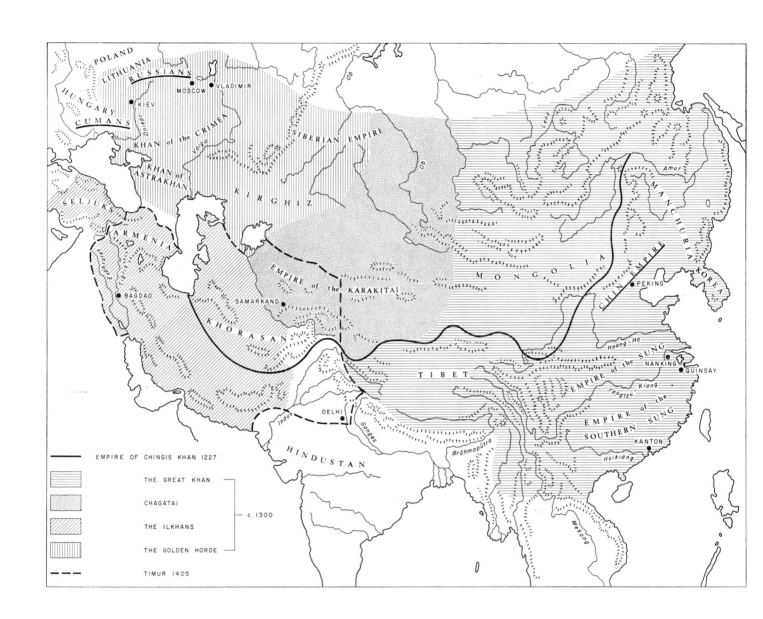

MONGOL EMPIRES

POLAND
LITHUANIA
RUSSIANS
HUNGARY
CUMANS
KHAN of the CRIMEA
KHAN of ASTRAKHAN
SELJUKS
ARMENIA
KHORASAN
SIBERIAN EMPIRE
KIRGHIZ
EMPIRE of the KARAKITAI
MONGOLIA
MANCHURIA
KOREA
CHIN EMPIRE
TIBET
HINDUSTAN
EMPIRE of the SUNG
EMPIRE of the SOUTHERN SUNG

MOSCOW
VLADIMIR
KIEV
BAGDAD
SAMARKAND
DELHI
PEKING
NANKING
QUINSAY
KANTON

Dniepr · Volga · Ob · Ob · Lena · Amur · Euphrates · Tigris · Indus · Ganges · Brahmaputra · Hoang-Ho · Yangtzu Kiang · Hsikiang · Mekong

EMPIRE OF CHINGIS KHAN 1227

THE GREAT KHAN

CHAGATAI   c. 1300

THE ILKHANS

THE GOLDEN HORDE

TIMUR 1405

After Heissig

108

NOTES ON THE TEXT

ABBREVIATIONS FOR THE PRINCIPAL WORKS QUOTED:

Marco Polo	*Reisen des Venezianers Marco Polo, bearbeitet von Dr Hans Lemke*, Hamburg, 1907
Yule-Cordier	*The Book of Ser Marco Polo the Venetian concerning the Kingdoms and Marvels of the East*, 2 vols., translated and edited in the notes by Colonel Sir Henry Yule. Third edition revised by Henri Cordier of Paris. London, 1903
Cordier	*Ser Marco Polo*. Notes and Addenda to Sir Henry Yule's edition, containing the results of recent research and discovery. London, 1920
Moule-Pelliot	*The Description of the World*, edited by A. C. Moule and Paul Pelliot, 2 vols. London, 1938. *Notes on Marco Polo*, by Paul Pelliot, 2 vols. Paris, 1958–63. Really a continuation of their joint work and in the same format. References therefore are to Moule-Pelliot I,i, I,ii, II,i, II,ii
Carpini/Risch	*Johann De Plano Carpini, Geschichte der Mongolen und Reisebericht 1245–47: übersetzt und erläutert von F. Risch*, Leipzig, 1930
von Rubruk/Risch	*Wilhelm von Rubruk, Reise zu den Mongolen 1253–55; übersetzt und erläutert von F. Risch*, Leipzig, 1934
Rockhill	W. W. Rockhill, *The Journey of William of Rubruk to the Eastern Parts of the World and Two Accounts of the Earlier Journey of John Plan de Carpine*. London (Hakluyt Society), 1900
Beazley	C. R. Beazley, *The Texts and Versions of John de Plano Carpini and William de Rubruquis*. London (Hakluyt Society), 1903
Haenisch	*Die Geheime Geschichte der Mongolen (aus einer mongolischen Niederschrift des Jahres 1420 von der Insel Kode's im Keluren-Fluss) erstmalig übersetzt und erläutert von E. Haenisch*, Leipzig 1948 (*zweite Auflage*)
Spuler	B. Spuler, *Die Mongolen in Iran*, Berlin 1955
Ettinghausen	R. Ettinghausen, *Arab Painting*, Cleveland (Ohio) and London, 1962
Ipsiroglu	M. S. Ipsiroglu, *Saray-Alben*, Wiesbaden 1964

[1] R. Ettinghausen, Some paintings in four Istanbul Albums, *Ars Orientalis* I, 1954, p. 101.

[2] M. Aurel Stein, *Sand-buried Ruins of Khotan*, London 1904, p. 232; Albert von Le Coq, *Von Land und Leuten in Ost-turkestan*, Leipzig 1928, pp. 15, 16; R. Ettinghausen, Chinese Representations of Central Asian Turks, *Beiträge zur Kunstgeschichte Asiens. Gedächtnisschrift Ernst Diez*, Istanbul 1963, pp. 208–222.

[3] The Osmanlis used for such albums a word borrowed from Arabic, *muraqqa'a*, which means more or less 'paste-work' or 'patchwork'. The stock of pictures in these albums was in fact assembled almost without selection from works of various periods and styles, and because on top of this individual pages were shuffled in the pagination without any consideration, the albums became serial collections in which even the initiated person can find his way only with great difficulty.

[4] The documents do not enable us to establish when these pages reached the Topkapu Museum. An opinion which is all too widespread in Turkish circles is that they found their way very early into the Sultan's Library, as early as the time of Mehmed the Conqueror. According to Ettinghausen the albums containing these volumes came to Turkey as plunder from the wars of Selim I (1512–20).

[5] In the Topkapu Museum at Istanbul a series of Saray albums has been opened to scientific study during the last ten years; of these, four volumes in particular (Hazine 2152, 2153, 2154, 2160) gave rise to much investigation and discussion: I. Stchoukine, Notes sur les peintures persanes du Serail de Stamboul, *Journal Asiatique* 226, 1935, pp. 117–140. O. Aslanapa, *Türkische Miniaturmalerei am Hofe Mehmet des Eroberers in Istanbul*, M. Loehr, The Chinese Elements in the Istanbul Miniatures, R. Ettinghausen, Some Paintings in Four Istanbul Albums, *Ars Orientalis* I, 1954, pp. 77–103, *id.*, On some Mongol Miniatures, *Kunst des Orients* III, 1959, pp. 44–65, *id.*, Persian Ascension Miniatures of the Fourteenth Century, *Accademia Nazionale dei Lincei*, Rome 1957, pp. 360–383, Ipsiroglu, S. Eyuboglu, *Fatih Albumuna*

bir bakīs, *Sur l'album du conquérant*, Istanbul Universitetesi Edebiyat Fakültesi Yayīnlarī 622.

Associated with the Istanbul albums were four more volumes in Germany (Diez A. Fol. 70–73), which reached the Royal Library, as it then was, along with many oriental manuscripts from the possession of the ambassador Friedrich Heinrich von Diez; they are now preserved in the Stiftung des Preussischen Kulturbesiztes, the Tübingen Depot of the State Library. M. S. Ipsiroglu, *Saray-Alben, Diez'sche Klebebände aus den Berliner Sammlungen*, Wiesbaden 1964. E. Kühnel, Malernamen in den Berliner 'Saray' Alben, in *Kunst des Orients* III, 1959.

The Tübingen and Istanbul Saray albums are very much alike in their make-up and content, and both doubtless belonged to a collection which, we may guess, was assembled in the time of Mehmed the Conqueror for the Sultan's Library. M. S. Ipsiroglu, Mongolische Miniaturen, *Pantheon* Part 5, 1964, 288–301.

6 *Manghol un niuca tobca'an (yüan c'ao pi-schi)*, Haenisch.

7 Mongke, Möngke, Mengku, Mangu.

8 von Rubruk/Risch and Rockhill.

9 Jinghiz, Chingis.

10 von Rubruk/Risch, *Rec.* (M. d'Avezac, Recueil de Voyages et de Mémoires de la Société de Géographie, 1839) IV, 359, p. 274. Rockhill, pp. 235–36.

11 F. Zarncke, II, 14. *Der Priester Johannes, 2 Abh. der Kgl. Sächsischen Gesellschaft der Wissenschaften*, Band VII, Leipzig 1883, as cited by F. Risch/P. Carpini, pp. 18 ff.

12 F. Zarncke, II, 21, as quoted in F. Risch/Carpini, p. 23.

13 The letter occurs in Matthew of Paris, as quoted in Carpini, p. 25. For Latin text see *Monumenta Germaniae Historica*, XXVIII, pp. 210–12.

14 Carpini/Risch.

15 von Rubruk/Risch, p. 3. Rockhill, introductory note pp. XXVII–XXIX.

16 Kipchak (the country of the Cumans) was subject to Batu and his son Sartakh, Hammer, *Geschichte der Goldenen Horde in Kiptschak*, Pesth 1840, C. A. Hartlebens Verlag. B. Spuler, *Die Goldene Horde* (Die Mongolen in Russland 1223–1502), Leipzig 1943. G. Vernadsky, *The Mongols in Russia* (vol. iii of *A History of Russia*, by G. Vernadsky and M. Karpovich) 1953.

17 von Rubruk/Risch, ch. XLVI, *Rec.* IV, 359, p. 274. Rockhill, pp. 238–39.

18 Carpini/Risch, p. 61. Beazley (Latin text), p. 47 and French translation in t'Serstevens, *Les Précurseurs de Marco Polo*, Paris 1959, p. 154.

19 Guyuk Khan's answer, which was discovered in 1920 with other important papers in the Vatican archives, is quoted in P. Carpini, p. 378. Rockhill, pp. 30 and 39, but our texts of Carpini do not contain the letter from Guyuk. This may be found, as translated from Papal records, in M. Pravdin, *The Mongol Empire*, London 1940, pp. 280–82.

20 von Rubruk/Risch, *Rec.* IV, 369, p. 292. Rockhill, pp. 248–51.

21 von Rubruk/Risch, *Rec.* IV, 355, p. 268. Rockhill, p. 250.

22 Ricold, IX, 15, as quoted in F. Risch/P. Carpini, 65, note 3.

23 Carpini/Risch, p. 71. Beazley (Latin text), p. 48 and French translation in t'Serstevens, p. 155.

24 Spuler, p. 238.

25 Spuler, p. 207. The sprinkling with wine, which according to Islamic belief is one of the forbidden drinks, was felt by the Mohammedans to be particularly offensive.

26 Spuler, pp. 209, 240.

27 Haenisch, Die Kulturpolitik des mongolischen Weltreiches, *Preussische Akademie der Wissenschaften, Vorträge und Schriften*, Heft II, Berlin, 1943, p. 28.

28 Haenisch, p. 23. Arthur Waley, *The Secret History of the Mongols and other Pieces*, p. 237.

29 Carpini/Risch, p. 66. Beazley (Latin text), pp. 47–48 and French translation in t'Serstevens pp. 154–55.

30 Carpini/Risch, pp. 68–70. Beazley (Latin text), p. 47 and French translation in t'Serstevens, pp. 154–55.

31 Max Müller, *Introduction to the Science of Religion* (1882), pp. 200–03.

32 von Rubruk/Risch, *Rec.* IV, 222, p. 40. Rockhill, pp. 58–59 and notes. Yule-Cordier, vol. I, p. 257. Moule-Pelliot, vol. I, 1. pp. 170–71.

33 Marco Polo, I, ch. 49, p. 178. Yule-Cordier, vol. I, p. 257. Moule-Pelliot, vol. I, 1, pp. 170–71.

34 von Rubruk/Risch, *Rec.* IV, 224, p. 42. Rockhill, pp. 60–61.

35 Marco Polo, I, ch. 58, p. 200. Yule-Cordier, vol. I, pp. 390–93. Moule-Pelliot, vol. I, 1, pp. 222–25.

36 Wassaf in D'Ohsson, *Histoire des Mongols*, II, p. 529.

37 von Rubruk/Risch, *Rec.* IV, 287, p. 161. Rockhill, pp. 58–59.

38 von Rubruk/Risch, *Rec.* IV, 315, p. 208. Rockhill, p. 184; other references to this wife, *ibid.*, pp. 171, 185–86, 206, 244–45.

39 von Rubruk/Risch, *Rec.* IV, 367, p. 288. Rockhill, pp. 245-46.

40 Marco Polo, I, ch. 58, p. 200. Yule-Cordier, vol. I, p. 301. Moule-Pelliot, vol. I, 1, p. 188.

41 von Rubruk/Risch, *Rec.* IV, 237, p. 75. Rockhill, pp. 82–83 and 192–96.

42 A. L. von Schloezer, *Abu Dalef, De Itinere Asiatico Commentarius* (1845, containing Qazvini's article on the Tartars), p. 32, as quoted in von Rubruk/Risch, *Rec.* IV, 238, p. 76, note 13.

43 W. Radloff, *Aus Sibirien* (2 vols. 1893), II 52–55.

44 Carpini/Risch, pp. 61–87. von Rubruk/Risch, *Rec.* IV, 319, Marco Polo, II, ch. 10. Rockhill, pp. 7, 10, 23 (Carpini); pp. 104, 188, 189 (Rubruk). Yule-Cordier, Vol. I, pp. 383, 385 note 4 (Marco Polo).

45 Huc, *Tartarie* I, 62, as quoted in von Rubruk/Risch.

46 Haenisch, p. IX.

47 von Rubruk/Risch, *Rec.* IV, 220–22, p. 36. Rockhill, p. 53 with notes.

48 von Rubruk/Risch, *Rec.* IV, 220–22, pp. 35–40. Rockhill, pp. 53–56.

49 von Rubruk/Risch, *Rec.* IV, 222, p. 39. Rockhill, *loc. cit.*

50 Ibn Battuta, II, 380. See H. A. R. Gibb, *The Travels of Ibn Battuta*, transl. vol. II (Hakluyt Society), 1962, p. 482.

⁵¹ von Rubruk/Risch, *Rec.* IV, 267, p. 123, Rockhill, pp. 57–58.
⁵² von Rubruk/Risch, IV, 222, p. 40. Rockhill, pp. 122–23.
⁵³ Carpini/Risch, p. 227. Rockhill, *loc. cit.*
⁵⁴ Carpini/Risch, p. 238. Rockhill, pp. 18–24 on three royal tents, pp. 21 ff. and pp. 37–39 on coronation tent of Guyuk.
⁵⁵ Marco Polo II, ch. 16, pp. 258–264. Yule-Cordier, vol. I pp. 403–06. Moule-Pelliot, vol. I, 1, p. 232. Yule points out that when Polo speaks of striped lions he means tigers, which had been forgotten by Europeans of his day, and that when he speaks of lynxes he means cheetahs.
⁵⁶ As quoted in Rockhill/William of Rubruk XIII, note 1. This is the chronicler Alberic de Bello Sacro (*Monumenta Germaniae Historica*, XXIII, pp. 631–95).
⁵⁷ Carpini/Risch, p. 55. Beazley (English text) p. 109.
⁵⁸ W. Radloff, I, 259, as quoted in F. Risch/P. Carpini, p. 55, note 1.
⁵⁹ von Rubruk/Risch, *Rec.* IV, 232, p. 60. Rockhill, p. 72.
⁶⁰ W. Radloff, I, 259, as quoted in von Rubruk/Risch, *Rec.* IV, 233, p. 62, note 11.
⁶¹ von Rubruk/Risch, *Rec.* IV, 233, p. 63. Rockhill, p. 74.
⁶² Carpini/Risch, p. 58. Rockhill, pp. 72–74.
⁶³ von Rubruk/Risch, *Rec.* IV, 232, p. 60. Rockhill, pp. 73–75.
⁶⁴ Carpini/Risch, pp. 88, 211; von Rubruk/Risch, *Rec.* 395, p. 335 Beazley (English text) p. 110.
⁶⁵ Marco Polo, I, ch. 54. Yule-Cordier, vol. I, pp. 260–63. Moule-Pelliot, vol. I, 1. p. 171.
⁶⁶ W. Radloff I, pp. 305–06, as quoted in F. Risch/P. Carpini, p. 91, note 7.
⁶⁷ Carpini/Risch, p. 88. Beazley (English text), pp. 110 and 120.
⁶⁸ Qazvini-Schloezer, p. 32, as quoted in F. Risch/P. Carpini, p. 88, note 1.
⁶⁹ W. Radloff I, 311, as quoted in F. Risch/P. Carpini, p. 88, note 1.
⁷⁰ Haenisch, p. 89.
⁷¹ Qazvini-Schloezer, p. 32, as quoted in F. Risch/P. Carpini, p. 88, note 2.
⁷² Ibn Battuta II, 362, as quoted in F. Risch/P. Carpini, p. 89, note 4. Gibb, transl. pp. 472–73.
⁷³ Carpini/Risch, p. 92. Beazley (English text), p. 110.
⁷⁴ W. Radloff, I, 312–13, as quoted in F. Risch/P. Carpini, p. 90, note 6.
⁷⁵ Carpini/Risch, p. 93. Beazley, *loc. cit.*
⁷⁶ von Rubruk/Risch, *Rec.* IV, 259, p. 108. Rockhill, pp. 248–51.
⁷⁷ Carpini/Risch, p. 105. Beazley (Latin text), p. 53 and French translation in t'Serstevens, p. 162.
⁷⁸ Haenisch, p. 116.
⁷⁹ Haenisch, p. 125.
⁸⁰ von Rubruk/Risch, *Rec.* IV, 227, p. 48. Rockhill, pp. 63–66.
⁸¹ Marco Polo II, ch. 16, pp. 258–264. Yule-Cordier, vol. I, pp. 397–400. Moule-Pelliot, vol. I, 1, pp. 227–29.
⁸² Marco Polo II, ch. 14, p. 256. Yule-Cordier, vol. I, p. 396. Moule-Pelliot, vol. I, 1, p. 227. Beazley (Latin text), pp. 62 and 66 and French translation in t'Serstevens, pp. 178–80.
⁸³ Spuler, p. 403, note 8.

⁸⁴ Carpini/Risch, p. 173, note 6. Beazley (Latin text), p. 64 and French translation in t'Serstevens, pp. 178–79.
⁸⁵ Carpini/Risch, p. 170. Beazley (Latin text), p. 65 and French in t' Serstevens, p. 179.
⁸⁶ Carpini/Risch, p. 173, note 7. Letter of Frederick II in Neaulmes, *Voyages faits en Asie*, Vol. VII, p. 30.
⁸⁷ Carpini/Risch, p. 174, note 10. Beazley (Latin text), p. 174. French in t' Serstevens, p. 179.
⁸⁸ Marco Polo, I, ch. 54. Yule-Cordier, vol. I, pp. 260–63. Moule-Pelliot, vol. I, 1, p. 213.
⁸⁹ Haenisch, p. 159, note 194.
⁹⁰ Carpini/Risch, p. 181, note 4. Beazley (Latin text), pp. 65–66 and French translation in t' Serstevens, p. 180.
⁹¹ The section on Mongol Law gives a very brief resumé from Spuler, where more detail will be found on pp. 373–398.
⁹² Marco Polo, I, ch. 7, p. 233. Yule-Cordier, vol. I, pp. 374–76. Moule-Pelliot, vol. I, 1, p. 213.
⁹³ Marco Polo, I, ch. 7, p. 235. Yule-Cordier, vol. I, pp. 412–15, Moule-Pelliot, vol. I, p. 256.
⁹⁴ Rashid-ed-Din as quoted in Hans Lemke, *Marco Polo*, p. 228, note 2.
⁹⁵ Marco Polo, I, ch. 58. Yule-Cordier, vol. I, pp. 298–300. Moule-Pelliot, vol. I, 1, pp. 186–87.
⁹⁶ von Rubruk/Risch, *Rec.* IV, 334, p. 239. Rockhill, pp. 21–22.
⁹⁷ Carpini/Risch, p. 238. Rockhill, p. 19.
⁹⁸ Rudi Paret, Textbelege zum islamischen Bildverbot, in *Das Werk des Künstlers, Hubert Schrade zum* 60. *Geburtstag*, pp. 36–48, Stuttgart 1961.
⁹⁹ Ettinghausen, p. 61.
¹⁰⁰ Ettinghausen, p. 82.
¹⁰¹ Ettinghausen, pp. 82–3.
¹⁰² Ettinghausen, pp. 67–103.
¹⁰³ Ettinghausen, plates on pp. 76, 77, 101.
¹⁰⁴ M. S. Ipsiroglu, Das Buch der Feste, in the monthly *Du*, Zürich, October 1963.
¹⁰⁵ cf. *Die Wiener Makamen des Hariri aus dem Jahre* 1334 (National Bibliothek, A F 9).
¹⁰⁶ *Ergebnisse der kgl. preussischen Turfan-Expeditionen. Die Buddhistische Spätantike in Mittelasien*, A. von le Coq/E. Waldschmidt VI, Neue Bildwerke II, Berlin MCMXXVIII.
¹⁰⁷ In the Vatican Library there is a second manuscript of a romance from the thirteenth century, which is also illustrated (the story of Bayad and Riyad MS. Ar. 368). Unfortunately both the text and the pictures of this manuscript are very incomplete. The miniatures are painted in the style of the Baghdad School and show here and there peculiarities of Christian book illustration of the Middle Ages. The place of origin of the manuscript is Morocco or perhaps even Spain. Further details: Ettinghausen pp. 125–30, plates on pp. 126, 127, 129.
¹⁰⁸ Alex. Baumgartner, *Geschichte der Weltliteratur* I, 3, 4, 1901 impression, p. 470.
¹⁰⁹ Ipsiroglu, p. 1, plates I and II.
¹¹⁰ Ettinghausen, Plate on p. 121.

[111] B. Gray, *Persian Painting*, Cleveland (Ohio) and London 1961. Plates on pp. 41, 42.

[112] Ipsiroglu, Plate XXVII.

[113] Ipsiroglu, pp. 15–32, Figs. 1–44.

[114] We do not nowadays possess very many of the manuscripts illustrated in Chinese-Mongol style. One of the earliest works of this kind is the *Tarikh-i Jahangušay* of Alâ-ed-Din 'Atâ Malik al Juvainî in the Bibliothèque Nationale, Paris (Suppl. pers. 205, dated 1290). From a somewhat later period are the *Jami-et-Tawarikh* illustrations of Rashid-ed-Din and the Tansuqnama of Ša'ban (Aya Sofya Library No. 3596 in Istanbul, dated 1313), the *Six Divans* of Mu'Izzî (London, India Office Ethé No. 912, dated 1313–15) and the *Garšaspnâme* (Istanbul, Topkapu Saray Museum, Hazine 674, dated 1354). Besides these illuminated manuscripts are only a few bundles of of loose Mongol miniatures torn from manuscripts which were found collected in different paste-albums in Istanbul and Tübingen and thus preserved for posterity. R. Ettinghausen has recently devoted a paper (On some Mongol Miniatures, *Kunst des Orients*, III, 1959, pp. 44–65) to the Mongol miniatures from one of these volumes (Hazine 2153).

[115] A series of such frontispieces is preserved from the manuscripts of the pre- and post-Mongol periods. The earliest comes from a manuscript of the tenth century found in Egypt (Vienna, Nationalbibliothek Chart. No. 25751; A. A. Grohmann and T. W. Arnold, *Denkmäler islamischer Buchkunst*. Munich 1929, Plate 4). The best known examples of such pictures are the first pages of the Pseudo-Galenic manuscript of the *Book of Antidotes* (*Kitâb-et-Tiryaq*, middle of the 13th century, Vienna, Nationalbibliothek A.F.10, Folio 1 recto; R. Ettinghausen, p. 91) and of the Harîrî Manuscript (*Maqamat des Harîrî* 1334, Vienna, Nationalbibliothek A.F.9, Folio 1 recto; R. Ettinghausen, p. 148). The picture of a ruler in the Diez paste-album (Diez A. Fol. 71, p. 46) in Tübingen belongs in this series too (Ipsiroglu p. 12, Plate IV).

[116] Ipsiroglu pp. 52 and 54.

[117] Ipsiroglu pp. 44–51.

[118] According to Dust Mohammed, the master Ahmed Musa illustrated not only the *Mi'rajnâme* mentioned, but an *Abû Sa'îdnâme*, a *Kalila and Dimna* and a History of Chingis Khan.

[119] The above-mentioned two representations of Paradise are today in two different places in the album (Hazine 2154, p. 61a and p. 121a); yet they belong together and once formed a complete page. Further detail on the iconography of these representations of the Ascension, in R. Ettinghausen, Persian Ascension Miniatures of the Fourteenth Century, *Accademia Nazionale dei Lincei*, Rome 1957, pp. 360–383.

[120] In a paper on the artists of the Saray albums (Topkapu Sarayîndaki dört Cönk, *Islam Tetkikleri Enstitüsü Dergisi* I, Istanbul 1953, pp. 73–89), Z. V. Togan has identified Mehmed Siyah Qalem with a painter named Mehmed Nakkas from Herat, of whose life and works his contemporary Khondemir gives the following account: 'He was an encyclopaedist of his time; he depicted strange events and notable figures on the pages of his life; he was a master in the arts of painting and illustration. Several times he tried to make Chinese porcelain, and after he had devoted much work to it with many experiments he succeeded in making a few dishes which were like Chinese porcelain; but their colour and quality were inferior to the models.'
Z. V. Togan's identification cannot be proved convincingly by this description, particularly since the name Mehmed was extremely common in the east. It remains for the present no more than a hypothesis.

[121] R. Ettinghausen, Some paintings in four Istanbul Albums, *Ars Orientalis* I, 1954, p. 102.

[122] Ipsiroglu, p. 15, Plate XI.

[123] Ipsiroglu, p. 16, Plate XII.

[124] E. Kühnel, Malernamen in den Berliner 'Saray' Alben, in *Kunst des Orients* III, 1959.

[125] Ipsiroglu, Figs. 96, 97, 102, 103, 104, 105, 106, 107.